GLASTONBURY
and the
Myths of Avalon

Yuri Leitch

First edition published in 2019.

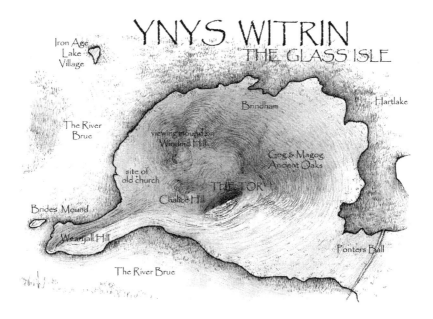

YNYS WITRIN

The original Brythonic name of Glastonbury,
translates as the Isle of Glass.

~ Other books by Yuri Leitch ~

*Gwyn: Ancient God of Glastonbury
and Key to the Glastonbury Zodiac*

* * *

The Ogham Year Wheel

* * *

*The Ogham Grove;
The Year Wheel of the Celtic/Druidic god
Ogma the Sun-Faced*

* * *

*The Terrestrial Alignments
of Katharine Maltwood and Dion Fortune*

* * *

Editor of

Signs & Secrets; of the Glastonbury Zodiac

* * *

The Maltwood Journal

* * *

Illustrator of

The Sacred Sites Oracle Cards

* * *

The Shamanic Medicine Oracle Cards

* * *

www.yurileitch.co.uk

~ CONTENTS ~

~APPENDICES ~

~ INTRODUCTION ~

This is not a book about the historical Arthur.

This is a book about the history of Arthurian romance and its very real significance to Glastonbury during medieval times. In many ways it is the Arthur of romance that people really love. The Arthur of history, busy fighting Saxons in the 6th century, is not the chivalrous Arthur of knights in armour, the Holy Grail, and Avalon; and he is not, and never was, the Arthur of Glastonbury.

The Arthur of Glastonbury is a myth created by the Benedictine order of Glastonbury Abbey; motivated by the many fascinating intrigues of their day; this is their story. The evidence for the real Arthur is very slim indeed. He was a cultural figure-head of the Dark Age Romano-British people; a symbol of hope in their struggle against the Anglo-Saxons. There probably was a great battle-leader who succeeded against the odds, for a generation or so during the early 500s, but by the time of the first Arthurian romance (circa 1136) his deeds had become exaggerated to those of super-human capabilities (beheading giants and conquering half of Europe, which of course never really happened). The Britons were eventually defeated by the Saxons and forced to retreat to the lands of Wales, Cornwall, and Brittany. But the twist is this, when William the Conqueror defeated Saxon England and created Norman England a great number of his followers and nobles were Breton (descendants of the British exiles who sang cultural stories about Arthur). The King Arthur of romance is thus a hero of Norman and Breton culture; no Anglo-Saxon ever considered him (their old enemy) worthy of a song. The Arthurian romances begin after the Battle of Hastings and its very special date that resonates with all day-dreaming school boys, 1066.

Stained-glass window of Saint David,
from Llangorwen, Ceredigion, Wales
(Image from Wiki Commons)

CHAPTER ONE
~ THE MYSTERIES OF SAINT DAVID ~

The history of Arthurian romance in Glastonbury begins with an important personality that has almost been completely erased (and deliberately so) from the town's memory; the patron saint of Wales, Saint David. He has been all but forgotten because the earliest evidence of the creation of Glastonbury Abbey is that Saint David was its founder and this is at odds with the much later 'tradition' that Joseph of Arimathea established the first church in Glastonbury. Thus the glamour of the Holy Grail mythology has almost succeeded in erasing the truer Celtic Church history of the town; and yet (ironically) the Saint David history is very important because it connects with Avallon in France and it incorporates a proto-grail archetype long before the town had any King Arthur significance.

Saint David was a 6th century contemporary of Arthur. He was a bishop of the Celtic Church and he was of royal blood (being a great-grandson of the famous British king, Cunedda). His main seat of power was situated upon the furthest west coast of Wales; St. David's Cathedral.

It is in the *Life of David* (the *Buchedd Dewi*), written around 1090 AD by a chap called Rhygyfarch, that David is described as building the first church in Glastonbury (40 years before any local history had been written down and about 160 years before the Joseph of Arimathea 'tradition' was invented).

Saint David is known as the patron saint of Wales but it would be more accurate to acknowledge him as the patron saint of the Britons (as much as Saint Patrick is of the Irish); even the Britons of Brittany had places named after him. In Brittany there were at least three places dedicated to '*Sant Dewi*' and their geographic locations are very interesting. Two of them, Saint-Divy and Saint-Yvi, are situated within the Finistère department of Brittany; and the third, Landivy, is situated in Mayenne (about 30 kilometres south of Mont-St-Michel). The important observation here is that, as with St. David's Cathedral in Pembrokeshire, Saint David is connected with the ends of the earth. Finistère is derived from the Latin *finis terrae* which literally means 'end of the earth' and it is akin to 'Land's End' in Cornwall. In medieval times (and earlier) pilgrimages to the ends of the earth, the furthest west to see the sun setting into the sea, were very popular; the most famous of which was the Camino de Santiago de Compostela (which will prove to be very important further on).

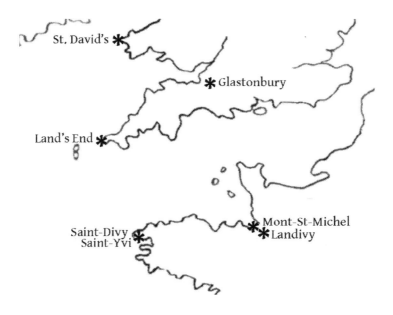

In the *Buchedd Dewi* Rhygyfarch describes '*Glastynburi*' as being the first of twelve monasteries founded by Saint David.

THE OLD STUFF
(pre-1066)

~ CELTIC IRON-AGE YNYS WITRIN ~

The isle of Ynys Witrin was probably a Druidic Nemeton. Its Iron Age lake-villages were connected to the Celtic Sea coastal trading network and the Somerset Levels were a natural division between two Celtic tribes; the Dobunni to the north and the Durotriges to the south (their immediate trading neighbours were the Dumnonii of Devon and Cornwall and the Silures of southern Wales.)

~ ROMAN TIMES ~

Every archaeological dig in Glastonbury has revealed the pottery and roof tiles of Roman occupation; including the top of the Tor and Glastonbury Abbey itself. There is even suggestive evidence by local archaeologists that there was once a Romano-British pagan temple on top of Glastonbury Tor; this would not be unexpected as the Somerset Levels are surrounded by Roman temples and Glastonbury Tor dominates the landscape for miles around. Britain was part of the Roman Empire from 43 AD until 410 AD. The empire actively suppressed Druidism and it did not tolerate Christianity until the beginning of the 4th century.

~ CELTIC CHRISTIANITY ~

The emperor Constantine made Christianity legal in 313 AD; thus the Celtic Church officially begins in the 4th century. The earliest known church in the British Isles was Candida Casa, the White House of Saint Ninian; which he established at Whithorn, in Galloway, circa 397 AD. The Celtic Church thrived in the 5th and 6th centuries under the missions of saints Patrick, Columba, David and others, but it was suppressed at the Synod of Whitby in 664 AD; the Saxons chose to follow the way of the Roman Church established in Canterbury by Augustine in 597 AD.

~ SAXON GLASTONBURY ~

According to the Anglo-Saxon Chronicle, in 682 AD the Saxon king, Centwine, pushed the last of the Britons to the sea (the Bristol Channel). The first stone church to be built at Glastonbury was during the reign of Ine, the Saxon king of Wessex between 688-726 AD.

* * *

The Popularity of Saint David

The original patron saint of England (as in the 'Angle-land' of the Anglo-Saxons) was Saint Edmund the Martyr of Bury St. Edmunds; but a sainted Saxon king meant very little to the Britons and Bretons that were descended from the Celtic Church of Saint David.

In 1081 AD William the Conqueror visited St. David's to pray. His visit gave the monastery royal recognition as a respected and holy place. Nine years later, Rhygyfarch (thought to have been a bishop of St. David's) wrote his *Buchedd Dewi,* which stated that Glastonbury had been the first of twelve monasteries that were established by David.

In 1115, King Henry I appointed a chap called Bernard to the position of bishop of St. David's. Bishop Bernard then petitioned the Pope to recognise David as a saint of the Roman Church (David wasn't yet, he was of the old suppressed Celtic Church). Five years later, in 1120, Pope Callixtus II consented and David became recognised as a saint by Rome. In 1123 the same Pope bestowed a papal privilege upon St. David's making it a centre of pilgrimage for the western world; stating that,

*'Two pilgrimages to St. David's is equal to one to Rome,
and three pilgrimages to one to Jerusalem'.*

Pilgrimage was big business. A new cathedral was quickly constructed and consecrated by Bishop Bernard in 1131. Pilgrims spent money at every church, chapel, and abbey that they visited on their way to their sacred destination. Glastonbury Abbey would be a prime location on the pilgrimage to St. David's; especially as it had been declared the very first monastery that David had built.

St. David's Cathedral, Pembrokeshire, Wales.

* * *

~ 1066 AND ONWARDS ~

1066 ~ *The Battle of Hastings; William the Conqueror is victorious; his half brother, Robert the Count of Mortain, fought by his side under the banner of the Archangel Michael (under the prayers of the Benedictine Order of Mont-St-Michel).*
1081 ~ *William the Conqueror visits St. David's to pray.*
1090 ~ *Rhygyfarch writes the Buchedd Dewi (Life of David).*
1115 ~ *Henry I appoints Bishop Bernard to St. David's.*
1120 ~ *Callixtus II makes David a saint of the Roman Church.*
1123 ~ *Callixtus II declares St. David's to be a sacred pilgrimage.*
1131 ~ *Bishop Bernard consecrates the new cathedral of St. David's.*

* * *

Whilst Bishop Bernard was busy building the new cathedral of St. David's the abbot of Glastonbury just happened to find the sacred foundation altar of Saint David; and he had the leading historian of the day (William of Malmesbury) stay at Glastonbury Abbey to write its history. Saint David's 'Sapphire Altar' is a prototype of the Holy Grail.

A medieval commemorative plaque at the British Museum
depicting Henry of Blois holding what is probably
Saint David's Sapphire Altar.
(Image from Wiki Commons)

Henry of Blois and the Antiquities of Glastonbury

Henry of Blois was abbot of Glastonbury, bishop of
Winchester, brother of Stephen, the King of England (and
many considered him to be the real power behind the
throne), and grandson of William the Conqueror. Even as a
young man he was known of as 'the Sage', and he was also
a brilliant business man. He was abbot of Glastonbury
between 1126 and 1171 AD.

*'He discovered, so the chroniclers relate, a precious
sapphire (probably a round porphyry slab of a 'gradale' type
used as a portable altar) which, according to tradition, had
been brought to Glastonbury by St David himself but had
been hidden during the long periods of instability in the
recesses of a door of St Mary's church. He adorned this
relic with gold, silver, and precious stones and had it
prominently displayed in the church where it remained as
an object of veneration for the rest of the monastery's
history.'*
(James P. Carley, *Glastonbury Abbey*)

Carley's choice of the word 'gradale' is very significant as the southern French slang for a *gradale* was *graalz*. This was understood, from at least the early part of the 13th century, to be the origin of the popular word *Grail*.

> *'720 AD ~ At this time a certain marvellous vision was revealed by an angel to a certain hermit in Britain concerning St. Joseph, the decurion who deposed from the cross the Body of Our Lord, as well as concerning the paten or dish in the which Our Lord supped with His disciples, whereof the history was written out by the said hermit and is called "Of the Graal" (de Gradali). Now, a platter, broad and somewhat deep, is called in French gradalis or gradale, wherein costly meats with their sauce are wont to be set before rich folk by degrees (gradatim) one morsel after another in divers orders, and in the vulgar speech it is called graalz...'*
> (The *Chronicon* of Hélinand, circa 1211-1223)

The above is not just coincidence. About 1129 Henry of Blois had William of Malmesbury write about his discovery of Saint David's Sapphire Altar; in the following description, taken from William's *Antiquities of Glastonbury*, I have high-lighted some significant statements by making them **bold**).

> *'CHAP. XXX – Concerning the Altar of St. David, commonly called 'the Sapphire'.*
>
> *We read in the life of St. David, the Archbishop of the Welsh, that when he was in the monastery of the Ross Valley ministering to a large number of brethren as abbot, one night an angel appeared to him saying: "Tomorrow gird thyself and bind on thy shoes, to go to Jerusalem. Thou shalt have with thee two of thine own household famed for their honesty, to wit, Elind and Paternus, as companions on thy journey, who will join thee tomorrow at an agreed place which I shall show thee in due time." Then the saint, without delay, after disposing of the*

useful articles in his tiny cell, and receiving the benediction of the brethren, commenced his journey at the peep of day, reached the spot agreed on and found the promised brethren. Thereupon they addressed themselves to their journey, not surrounded by the pomp of satellites, but rich in unity of soul. None of them was lord, none servant, but they were comrades all three.

As they entered foreign provinces, St. David became so graced with the gift of tongues, that they needed no interpreter among the barbarians. And as they drew near their desired haven, on the night preceding their arrival, an angel appeared **to the Patriarch of Jerusalem, saying "Three Catholic men are coming from the ends of the West,** whom thou shalt receive gladly, giving them hospitality freely, and thou shalt consecrate me their bishop." The patriarch thereupon, when he had understood the vision, joyfully carried out the angelic commands to the saints when they arrived, and, when he had blessed them, he said: "The power of the Jews is growing stronger against the Christians; they harass us and drive far the Faith. Pray, therefore, and preach day by day, that their violence may be checked and abated, knowing, that **the Christian faith has spread to the ends of the West, and that its praises are sung to the ends of the earth".** And they obey the command by persisting in preaching, and, the archbishop's prophecy having been accepted, they convert the infidels, strengthen the weak, and, having finished their task, they begin to make ready to return homewards. **Then the patriarch enriched the venerable father David with four gifts; namely, a consecrated altar, on which the Lord's body had been sacrificed, which was mighty in innumerable virtues,** also a remarkable bell, a staff, a tunic woven of gold, all of which exhibit brilliance by the glorious miracles they work. "But", quoth the patriarch, "as these will be burdensome to you on your journey, when ye have reached home I will send them on to you." They then bade farewell to the patriarch, and finally reached home and waited for *the promise of the holy man to be fulfilled. At length they received the presents, addressed to them by messengers; David in the monastery of Langemelech, Paternus and Elind in their own monasteries. Hence 'twas commonly said thereabouts that the gifts came from Heaven. But* **Saint David, desiring that such a treasure should have a worthy custodian when he had gone, bequeathed the stone to the church of Glastonbury** *whilst he was yet alive, which church he embraced with a wonderful affection, because of the venerable antiquity of the spot, and especially because the relics of Saint Patrick and other saints were treasured there, as may be plainly read and proved in his Acts.* **The said altar is therefore exhibited to this day in the church of Glastonbury in memory of the said saint**, *not preserved by human effort but by Divine providence, who, amid the constant whirl of change, and the succession of kings and kingdoms, amid the heaviest storms of warfare, when all else had been overturned or removed, continued to keep the greedy hands of foes aloof from this treasure.*

The case in which St. David received the said stone is treasured with fitting honour to this day in his episcopal see. When the oft-mentioned stone, which had been hidden through fear in time of war, had lain lost for a long time in the old days, **Henry, Bishop of Winchester, of pious memory, who was also Abbot of Glastonbury, found it in a certain doorway of the Church of St. Mary**, *and adorned it magnificently with gold and silver and precious stones, as it is now.'*

(William of Malmesbury, *The Antiquities of Glastonbury*)

The most important thing in the above quote is the description of the Sapphire Altar as,

'... a consecrated altar, on which the Lord's body had been sacrificed, which was mighty in innumerable virtues.'

The most important thing about the Holy Grail is that it was miraculously sanctified by the blood, sweat (and other bodily fluids), of Jesus; either during or just after his crucifixion. David's Sapphire Altar, being a sacred relic from Jerusalem upon which the Lord had been sacrificed, is thus a proto-grail that pre-dates the very first description of the Holy Grail (by Chrétien de Troyes; in his *Perceval ou le Conte du Graal*) by at least fifty years. This holy altar stone from Jerusalem, upon which Jesus had been sacrificed, was the most celebrated and worshipped relic of Glastonbury Abbey for all of the pilgrims visiting on their way to St. David's (and if they wanted to equal a pilgrimage to Jerusalem they had to pay homage to it on three separate occasions – 'ker-ching' the sound-effect of the abbey cash register).

I'll talk about the importance of Jerusalem in the next chapter but for now I want to point out the references to '**the ends of the West**' (which occurs twice), and the meaningful '**ends of the earth**'. As we have already observed St. David's cathedral is situated at the end of the earth (as far as south Wales is concerned) and Saint-Divy and Saint-Yvi of Brittany are situated within the department of Finistère (the end of the earth). The most famous pilgrimage to the end of the earth is that of the Camino de Santiago de Compostela (which concludes at Cape Finisterre on the west coast of Spain); this pilgrimage route is also known as The Way of Saint James. Probably the most sacred starting place for medieval pilgrims in France, setting off on the long walk to Cape Finisterre, was the religious cult centre of Mary Magdalene, Vézelay.

Vézelay was the spiritual centre of France and it was an influential rallying place for the first, second, and third crusades. More importantly it was part of a large forested area known as the Avallonnais; named after the town of Avallon. In short, in France, the sacred pilgrimage to 'the end of the earth' began in the Avallonnais (as the sacred pilgrimage to St. David's began at Glastonbury).

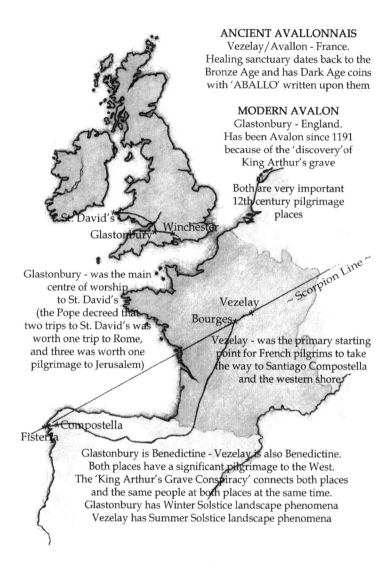

ANCIENT AVALLONNAIS
Vezelay/Avallon - France.
Healing sanctuary dates back to the Bronze Age and has Dark Age coins with 'ABALLO' written upon them

MODERN AVALON
Glastonbury - England.
Has been Avalon since 1191 because of the 'discovery' of King Arthur's grave

Both are very important 12th century pilgrimage places

Glastonbury - was the main centre of worship to St. David's (the Pope decreed that two trips to St. David's was worth one trip to Rome, and three was worth one pilgrimage to Jerusalem)

Scorpion Line

Vezelay
Bourges

Vezelay - was the primary starting point for French pilgrims to take the way to Santiago Compostella and the western shore

Compostella
Fisterra

Glastonbury is Benedictine - Vezelay is also Benedictine. Both places have a significant pilgrimage to the West. The 'King Arthur's Grave Conspiracy' connects both places and the same people at both places at the same time. Glastonbury has Winter Solstice landscape phenomena Vezelay has Summer Solstice landscape phenomena

At the same time as the early popularity of the Pope-sanctioned pilgrimage to St. David's, Geoffrey of Monmouth was busy writing his *History of the Kings of Britain;* which he completed around 1136 AD. His book is the very first romance about King Arthur and in it Geoffrey states that Saint David was King Arthur's uncle.

Confusingly, *The History of the Kings of Britain* is not a history book, it is a work of fiction. So many well-loved elements of Arthurian romance begin with this story of the British kings; for the first time ever we are given mention of Merlin, Queen Guinevere, Mordred, Excalibur, and the Isle of Avalon. Geoffrey of Monmouth's first mention of Saint David is during a great festive gathering that King Arthur holds at the City of Legions (Caerleon-upon-Usk) with royal visitors in attendance from all over Europe,

'On the fourth day all those who in the office which they held had done Arthur any service were called together and each rewarded with a personal grant of cities, castles, archbishoprics, bishoprics and other landed possessions. Then the saintly Dubricius, who for a long time had wanted to live as a hermit, resigned from his position as Archbishop. David, the King's uncle, whose way of life had afforded an example of unblemished virtue to those whom he had instructed in the faith, was consecrated in his place.'

(Geoffrey of Monmouth, *History of the King's of Britain*)

The above quote has David become the Archbishop of the Britons; which is the highest religious position in Arthur's kingdom. Geoffrey's second mention of Saint David follows shortly after his account of Arthur's tragic ending,

*'Arthur himself, **our renowned King**, was mortally wounded and was carried off to the Isle of Avalon, so that his wounds might be attended to. He handed the crown of Britain over to his cousin Constantine, the son of Cador Duke of Cornwall: this in the year 542 after our Lord's incarnation.*

... It was then, too, that David, the most holy Archbishop of the City of Legions, died in the town of Menevia, inside his own abbey, which he loved more than all the other monasteries of his diocese...'

(Geoffrey of Monmouth, *History of the Kings of Britain*)

Although it may not seem of much significance at the moment, the description 'our renowned King' will prove to be very important in the next chapter.

Geoffrey's book is the earliest known evidence for the Isle of Avalon. His book was written in Latin and his original spelling of the Isle of Avalon was *Insula Avallonis*. Avallonis clearly bears a stronger similarity to Avallonnais (the area of Vézelay and Avallon in France) than it does to the modern spelling of Avalon. It must also be observed that Geoffrey's story, whilst describing a great many locations (like Tintagel, St. David's, Caerleon, Totnes, Winchester, and even Bath which is but a days horse ride from Glastonbury) never mentions the Somerset town or its abbey at all, never mind equating it with his *'Insula Avallonis'*. Almost fifteen years later, in his *Vita Merlini* (Life of Merlin), Geoffrey described King Arthur's ending a second time and completely dropped *Insula Avallonis* and replaced it with *'Insula Pomorum'* (Island of Apples); clearly intending it to be seen as a spiritual otherworld like the classical Garden of the Hesperides.

*'The Island of Apples which men call 'The Fortunate Isle' gets its name from the fact that it produces all things of itself; the fields there have no need of the ploughs of the farmers and all cultivation is lacking except what nature provides. Of its own accord it produces grain and grapes, and apple trees grow in its woods from the close-clipped grass. The ground of its own accord produces everything instead of merely grass, and people live there a hundred years or more. There nine sisters rule by a pleasing set of laws those who come to them from our country. She who is first of them is more skilled in the healing art, and excels her sisters in the beauty of her person. **Morgen** is her name, and she has learned what useful properties all the herbs contain, so that she can cure sick bodies. She also knows an art by which to change her shape, and to cleave*

the air on new wings like Daedalus; when she wishes she is at Brest, Chartres, or Pavia, and when she will she slips down from the air onto your shores. And men say that she has taught mathematics to her sisters, Monronoe, Mazoe, Gliten, Glitonea, Gliton, Tyronoe, Thitis; Thitis best known for her cither. Thither after the battle of Camlan we took the wounded Arthur, guided by Barinthus to whom the waters and the stars of heaven were well known. With him steering the ship we arrived there with the prince, and Morgen received us with fitting honour, and in her chamber she placed the king on a golden bed and with her own hand she uncovered his honourable wound and gazed at it for a long time. At length she said that health could be restored to him if he stayed with her for a long time and made use of her healing art. Rejoicing, therefore, we entrusted the king to her and returning spread our sails to the favouring winds.'

(Taliesin reporting to Merlin; in Geoffrey of Monmouth's *Vita Merlini*)

About five years after Geoffrey of Monmouth finished writing his *Vita Merlini*, a Norman French poet called Wace completed his own great work, *Roman de Brut*. Wace's romance is, for the most part, a translation of Geoffrey's *History of the King's of Britain*; but Wace made more than a few important changes. Firstly, he added what has become one of Arthur's most iconic things, the Round Table (which was not mentioned in Geoffrey's original story). Secondly, Wace turned Geoffrey's Latin *Avallonis* into the common 'Avalon'. Thirdly, and most importantly for this chapter, Wace made no mention of Saint David at all; King Arthur's uncle was erased from the story completely. Why?

The popularity of the pilgrimage to St. David's did not last very long as it was interrupted by the turmoil of England's first civil war; a period of history that is remembered as The Anarchy turned England into a very real Arthurian wasteland.

The pilgrimages to St. David's really began to take off after Bishop Bernard consecrated his new cathedral in 1131. For four years abbot Henry of Blois and the monks of Glastonbury were able to promote David's Sapphire Altar, the bejewelled sacred relic from Jerusalem sanctified by Christ's blood at the crucifixion, but then The Anarchy began and Henry of Blois became tangled up in the whole mess of it all from the beginning. In 1135 King Henry I died and the abbot of Glastonbury's brother, Stephen, seized the throne of England. Henry's chosen heir had been his daughter, the Empress Matilda, but Stephen and his supporters were not going to let the crown go to a woman. England and Normandy fell into chaos with some nobles supporting King Stephen and others supporting the Empress. Henry of Blois, as an important man of god (he was also bishop of Winchester) had to be seen to be trying to hold the peace but to the followers of Matilda he was seen as the corrupt brother of an unlawful king.

'In spite of all these virtues Henry's character [Henry of Blois] *did have its shortcomings. His love of fine things, for example, extended well beyond the limit tolerable in a man vowed to monastic poverty and the ascetic St. Bernard of Clairvaux contemptuously labelled him variously a rival pope, the old wizard of Winchester, and the whore of Winchester. Even with, or perhaps as a result of, his redoubtable administrative abilities and royal connections he managed to get himself embroiled in complex and sometimes unsavory political intrigues and on occasion military skirmishes. The contemporary chronicler, Henry of Huntingdon, referred to him with contempt as 'a new kind of monster, a monk-soldier'. Nevertheless, in the twelfth century what Glastonbury needed very badly was a strong patron, an abbot capable of reorganizing the financial life of the institution. For this reason, then, few abbots could have been more suitable at the time than Henry of Blois, who in the local context at least well deserved the lavish praises heaped upon him by the Glastonbury writers.'*
(James P. Carley, *Glastonbury Abbey*)

As to whether Henry of Blois was seen as a good person or not depended upon whose side of the civil war one was on (King Stephen's or Empress Matilda's) every person has their political preference. An over-looked and most curious intrigue of The Anarchy is how close it came to Glastonbury

Abbey; and the name of the nobles that lived there.

Signage from the site of Castle Cary.

The Castle was besieged twice by King Stephen, in 1138 and 1153, during the minor civil war which arose through a baronial dispute about his right to the throne. At that time the Lords of Cary were the Norman war lords, the de Percevals (who subsequently changed their name to Lovel). They supported the claim to the throne of the future Henry II. The Lovels were the Lords of Cary for some 250 years until the main line of this branch of the family died out in the middle of the 14th century.

Information from the Castle Cary sign.

Lets state this very clearly: Castle Cary was the castle of the Perceval family. In Arthurian Romances that were not yet written at the time of The Anarchy it would be the character Sir Percival that would become famed in the story of the Grail. From the site of Castle Cary, the one thing that dominates the view, fourteen miles away upon the horizon, is Glastonbury Tor, below which sat the abbey and its proto-grail, the Sapphire Altar of Saint David.

* * *

~ THE ANARCHY ~
(1135 – 1153)

1126 ~ *Henry of Blois became abbot of Glastonbury.*

1128 (circa) ~ *Henry of Blois found Saint David's Sapphire Altar.*

1129 ~ *William of Malmesbury was employed by Henry of Blois to write the 'Antiquities of Glastonbury' promoting Saint David's proto-grail from Jerusalem.*

1131 ~ *Bishop Bernard consecrated the new cathedral of St. David's; then only four years of sacred pilgrimage followed before the kingdom was interrupted by civil war.*

1135 ~ *Henry I died; his nephew, Stephen of Blois, the younger brother of Abbot Henry of Blois, seized the throne of England; this marks the beginning of The Anarchy (Henry I's chosen heir was his daughter, the Empress Matilda). King Stephen held the throne of England until 1154 but the land was wasted by constant civil war (not an environment harmonious to sacred pilgrimage).*

1136 ~ *Geoffrey of Monmouth's 'History of the Kings of Britain' is the first full life romance of King Arthur (and it gives the very first mention of Guinevere, Merlin, Excalibur, and Avalon); Geoffrey states that Saint David was King Arthur's uncle and archbishop of Arthur's entire kingdom.*

1138 ~ *King Stephen lays siege upon Castle Cary.*

1139 ~ *Empress Matilda invades England.*

1141 ~ *The Battle of Lincoln; King Stephen is captured but is later released.*

1142 ~ *the Siege of Oxford; Empress Matilda escapes across the frozen River Thames.*

1148 ~ *Empress Matilda returns to Normandy.*

1150 ~ *Geoffrey of Monmouth completes his 'Vita Merlini'.*

1153 ~ *King Stephen lays siege upon Castle Cary a second time.*

1153 ~ *The Treaty of Wallingford establishes peace at last.*

1154 ~ *King Stephen dies, Henry, the son of Empress Matilda, becomes Henry II, the first Angevin king of England.*

1155 ~ *Wace completes his 'Roman de Brut'; erasing Saint David from the story of King Arthur.*

* * *

That Wace chose to remove Saint David from the story of King Arthur may signify that he was a Norman on the political side of Empress Matilda (removing Saint David because he was perceived as an intrigue of Henry of Blois and his brother) or, alternatively, after eighteen years of civil war the pilgrimage to St. David's had fallen from memory and David's importance had been forgotten.

That the Grail was looked for (in the Arthurian romances) to heal the wasteland is more than apt considering that during the time of The Anarchy the struggles literally scorched the landscape; burning lands around castles to starve the inhabitants was a common and devastating strategy that ruined the land for generations. One can also add to this mix the proto-grail lost and forgotten; only by finding it again would the land be restored. Real history that may have inspired the Grail stories?

Arthur in Glastonbury

During the final years of The Anarchy another writer was busy adding an intrigue to Glastonbury's melting-pot. Caradoc of Llancarfan's *Life of Gildas* is the earliest evidence for Arthur being connected to Glastonbury. It is not known for certain when Caradoc's short biography of Saint Gildas was written; it may have been as early as the 1140s although most scholars accept a date of around 1155 AD. Caradoc of Llancarfan was a contemporary of Geoffrey of Monmouth and they appear to have known each other; and both of their writings are works of fiction. An earlier *Life of Gildas* claimed that Gildas was buried in Brittany but Caradoc's later *Life* claims Gildas was buried at Glastonbury (indeed, this was his purpose for writing it). It is thought that Caradoc may have been a monk or cleric of Glastonbury; if this is true then he was writing under the watchful eye of his abbot, Henry of Blois.

Caradoc's *Life of Gildas* tells the story of King Melvas abducting Queen Guinevere and keeping her as his prisoner in Glastonbury until King Arthur arrives with an army to rescue her.

'While St. Gildas was thus persevering, devoting himself to fastings and prayers, pirates came from the islands of the Orcades, who harassed him by snatching off his servants from him when at their duties, and carrying them to exile, along with spoils and all the furniture of their dwelling. Being thereby exceedingly distressed, he could not remain there any longer: he left the island, embarked on board a small ship, and, in great grief, put in at Glastonia, at the time when king Melvas was reigning in the summer country. He was received with much welcome by the abbot of Glastonia, and taught the brethren and the scattered people, sowing the precious seed of the heavenly doctrine. It was there that he wrote the history of the kings of Britain. Glastonia, that is, the glassy city, which took its name from 'glass', is a city that had its name originally in the British tongue. It was besieged by the tyrant Arthur with a countless multitude on account of his wife Gwenhwyfar, whom the aforesaid wicked king had violated and carried off, and brought there for protection, owing to the asylum afforded by the invulnerable position due to the fortifications of thickets of reed, river, and marsh. The rebellious king had searched for the queen throughout the course of one year, and at last heard that she remained there. Thereupon he roused the armies of the whole of Cornubia and Dibneria; war was prepared between the enemies.

When he saw this, the abbot of Glastonia, attended by the clergy and Gildas the Wise, stepped in between the contending armies, and in a peaceable manner advised his king, Melvas, to restore the ravished lady. Accordingly she who was to be restored, was restored in peace and good will. When these things were done, the two kings gave to the abbot a gift of many domains...'
(Caradoc of Llancarfan, *Life of Gildas*)

Caradoc's story served two purposes: one, to claim that St. Gildas was buried at Glastonbury and two, to claim various land rights for the abbey (the '*many domains*' mentioned in the last line of the quote on the opposite page). The interesting thing about this story of Melvas the king of the 'summer country' abducting Guinevere and Arthur having to rescue her a year later, is that it is a common Winter King verses Summer King year-battle that is told in many variations in Celtic and Arthurian mythology (I'll go into this in more detail in Appendix II). It is yet another intrigue from Glastonbury during the abbacy of Henry of Blois. During the 1160s Henry of Blois was involved in the struggles between King Henry II and Thomas Beckett. In 1171 Henry of Blois died. Thirteen years later his beloved abbey was destroyed, burnt down by The Great Fire of 1184; but potent Arthurian seeds had been sewn.

Henry of Blois, abbot of Glastonbury.

* * *

Largest 'pyramid' was 26ft high

Smallest 'pyramid' was 18ft high

The 'Leaden Cross' was found attached to a stone slab 7ft below the ground

GERALD of WALES

the monks dug 18ft deep

MARGAM CHRONICLE

Says one grave known about and looked for

Says three graves found by accident

This illustration is to scale
(based on the monks being 6ft tall)
so that the height of the 'pyramids'
and the depth the monks dug
can be appreciated.

CHAPTER TWO
~ THE MYSTERIES OF KING ARTHUR ~

Henry II died in 1189, about five years after the Great Fire of Glastonbury Abbey. The abbey, like a phoenix, had to rebirth itself from its own ashes; and it did so. The new king of England was Henry's son, Richard the Lionheart; that most dedicated crusading warrior (and he was steeped in Arthurian lore).

In the year 1187 the enigmatic Islamic leader, Saladin, captured Jerusalem. The Christian world responded with the Third Crusade. In 1190 Richard the Lionheart spent quite a length of time at Vézelay, in the Avallonnais, with Philip II, the king of France, planning the Third Crusade.

What now follows is true recorded history and yet it sounds like fiction; it is not, it is very real. In 1191, on his way to the Holy Land, Richard I stopped at Sicily. He gave Tancred, the king of Sicily, a sword that he claimed was King Arthur's sword Excalibur. This very same year the monks of Glastonbury made their claim of discovering King Arthur's grave; and the abbot of Glastonbury, at that time, was one Henry of Sully, King Richard's own nephew.

Vézelay, the fortified hill-top town, in the Avallonnais.
The French cult centre of Mary Magdalene.
Here Richard the Lionheart and the king of France
prepared for the Third Crusade.

~ THE CRUSADES ~

~~~ THE FIRST CRUSADE ~~~

1075 ~ Moslem Turks capture Jerusalem.
1095 ~ The Council of Clermont; Pope Urban II called for the First Crusade.
1099 ~ Crusaders capture Jerusalem; end of the First Crusade. The Christian kingdom of Jerusalem is founded.
1099 ~ Foundation of the Knights of St John.
1100 ~ Baldwin I is crowned King of Jerusalem.
1119 ~ Foundation of the Knights Templar.
1128 ~ The Knights Templar are licensed as a military order, by Pope Honorius II.

~~~ THE SECOND CRUSADE ~~~

1147 ~ The Second Crusade is announced by Pope Eugene III
1149 ~ End of the Second Crusade.

~~~ THE THIRD CRUSADE ~~~

1187 ~ Saladin captures Jerusalem.
1189 ~ Beginning of the Third Crusade.
1190 ~ Richard the Lionheart at Vézelay, in the Avallonnais.
1191 ~ King Arthur's grave hoax at Glastonbury; Richard the Lionheart gives Excalibur to King Tancred of Sicily on route to the Holy Land.
1192 ~ End of the Third Crusade.
1193 ~ Saladin dies.

~~~ THE ALBIGENSIAN CRUSADE ~~~

1209 ~ The Albigensian Crusade initiated by Pope Innocent III; to eliminate the Cathars.
1229 ~ End of the Albigensian Crusade.

~~~ THE END OF CRUSADING IN THE HOLY LAND ~~~

1291 ~ The fall of Acre; and the end of crusading against the Saracens.

* * *

The intrigue of King Arthur's grave at Glastonbury is accepted by most scholars to have been a hoax; but it is a fascinating story with many repercussions. Probably the most enduring repercussion is that it officially established Glastonbury as being the mythical realm of Avalon.

The 'cross of lead' that the monks are said to have found in King Arthur's grave is the only evidence that Glastonbury is Avalon (everything else, the supportive evidence, comes afterwards by later writers wanting to establish it as a fact). We have no first-hand eye-witness account of the discovery of Arthur's grave. The earliest account was written by Gerald of Wales a year or two after the event. As it is such an important piece of information it is worth quoting in full:

'Now the body of King Arthur, which legend has feigned to have been transferred at his passing, as it were in ghostly form, by spirits to a distant place and to have been exempt from death, was found in these our days at Glastonbury deep down in the earth and encoffined in a hollow oak between two stone pyramids erected long ago in the consecrated graveyard, the site being revealed by strange and almost miraculous signs; and it was afterwards transported with honour to the Church and decently consigned to a marble tomb. Now in the grave there was found a cross of lead, placed under a stone and not above it, as is now customary, but fixed on the lower side. This cross I myself have seen; for I have felt the letters engraved thereon, which do not project or stand out, but are turned inwards toward the stone. They run as follows.

HERE LIES BURIED **THE RENOWNED KING ARTHUR** WITH GUINEVERE HIS SECOND WIFE **IN THE ISLE OF AVALON**

Now in regard to this there are many things worthy of note. For he had two wives, the last of whom was buried with him, and her bones were found together with his, but separated from them as thus; two parts of the tomb, to wit, the head, were allotted to the bones of the man, while the remaining third towards the foot contained the bones of the woman in a place apart; and there was found a yellow tress of woman's hair still retaining its colour and its freshness; but when a certain monk snatched it and lifted it with a greedy hand, it straight away all of it fell into dust. Now whereas there were certain indications in their writings that the body would be found there, and others in the letters engraven upon the pyramids, though they were much defaced by their extreme age, and others again were given in visions and revelations vouchsafed to good men and religious, yet it was above all King Henry II of England that most clearly informed the monks, as he had heard from an ancient Welsh bard, a singer of the past, that they would find the body at least sixteen feet beneath the earth, not in a tomb of stone, but in a hollow oak. And this is the reason why the body was placed so deep and hidden away, to wit, that it might not by any means be discovered by the Saxons who occupied the island after his death, whom he had so often in his life defeated and almost utterly destroyed; and for the same reason those letters, witnessing to the truth, that were stamped upon the cross, were turned inwards towards the stone, that they might at that time conceal what the tomb contained, and yet in due time and place might some day reveal the truth.

Now the place which is now called Glaston, was in ancient times called the isle of Avalon, that is as it were an isle, covered with marshes, wherefore in the British tongue it was called Ynis Avallon, that is 'the apple-bearing isle'. Wherefore Morganis, a noble matron and the ruler and lady of those parts, who moreover was kin by blood to King Arthur, carried him away after the war of Camlan to the island that is now called Glaston that she might heal his wounds. It was also once called 'Inis gutrin' in the British tongue, that is, the glassy isle, wherefore when the Saxons afterwards came thither they called the place Glastingeburi. For 'Glas' in their language has the same meaning as 'uitrum' while 'buri' means 'castrum' or 'civitas'.

You must also know that the bones of Arthur thus discovered were so huge that the words of the poet seemed to be fulfilled:

"And he shall marvel at huge bones
In tombs his spade has riven'

*For his shank-bone, when placed against that of the tallest man in that place and planted in the earth near his foot, reached **(as the Abbot showed us)** a good three inches above his knee. And the skull was so large and capacious as to be a portent or prodigy; for the eye-socket was a good palm in width. Moreover, there were ten wounds or more, all of which were scarred over, save one larger than the rest, which had made a large hole.'*

(Gerald of Wales, circa 1193)

35

There is much to question in regards to the truth about King Arthur's grave at Glastonbury and thus Glastonbury being Avalon. I'll present here some critically important observations; firstly, the writing upon the cross of lead is clearly influenced by the fictional *History of the Kings of Britain* by Geoffrey of Monmouth (written in 1136 and discussed in the previous chapter).

* Word for word Geoffrey of Monmouth: Gerald of Wales declared that the cross of lead was inscribed with the description '**renowned King Arthur**' which is clearly taken from Geoffrey of Monmouth's *History* (see page 20). The cross also mentions Guinevere and the Isle of Avalon; both of which were first introduced to the world by Geoffrey of Monmouth. Further on in his description, when describing Glastonbury as 'Ynis Avallon' Gerald also describes the lady Morganis (the lady Morgen was first introduced to the world in Geoffrey of Monmouth's *Vita Merlini* (see page 21). Geoffrey's *History* was already fifty years old by the time the monks claimed to discover King Arthur's grave and it was believed to be true history by many people.

* King Arthur was not a 'King': The earliest writing about Arthur (the Nennius writings) call Arthur 'the warrior' and '*dux bellorum*' (a battle-leader) but never a 'King'. Nennius describes Arthur leading the kings (plural) of Britain into battle but Arthur himself is just their battle-leader. It is only by Geoffrey of Monmouth in his 12th century fiction, written almost six-hundred years after Arthur lived, that Arthur becomes a '*Rex*' (King). This is important because it is most unlikely that if the grave was a genuine 6th century burial that Arthur's people would have inscribed 'renowned king' upon his memorial cross.

* 12th century style writing: Some people look to the assumed primitive style of writing on the cross of lead to argue that it is far older than the 12th century but this does not stand up to scrutiny as the Sagittarius inscription of the Stoke-sub-Hamdon tympanum, in Somerset, is of the 12th century and it is very similar in its jumbled and erratic style.

12th century *SAGITTARIUS* inscription from Stoke-sub-Hamdon, Somerset. Compare with the style of writing upon the cross of lead shown on the front cover of this book and on page 1. The capital letter As even have the same characteristic cross-bar.
The cross of lead from King Arthur's grave is 12th century in style.

* The cross does not say what it should say: According to Gerald of Wales, our earliest eye-witness, the inscription on the cross said,

HERE LIES BURIED THE RENOWNED KING ARTHUR WITH
GUINEVERE HIS SECOND WIFE
IN THE ISLE OF AVALON

But the cross of lead on the front cover of this book (and on page 1) does not mention Guinevere at all, never mind that she was Arthur's second wife. The cross on the front cover of this book is shown in many books but it cannot be a true depiction of the original cross of lead (that or Gerald of Wales was shown another cross entirely). The well known version on the front cover reads,

HIC JACET SEPULTUS INCLITUS REX ARTURIUS
IN INSULA AVALONIA

* * *

HERE LIES BURIED THE RENOWNED KING ARTHUR
IN THE ISLE OF AVALON

The well known image of the cross on the front cover of this book is actually from an illustration in Camden's *Britannia* of 1607. Nobody knows what the original cross of lead looked like; but it should mention Guinevere.

   * What really happened?: In 1184 Glastonbury Abbey burnt down; very little was left standing. The king, Henry II, assisted financially with its repair and rebuilding but he died in 1189 and his son Richard the Lionheart wasn't interested in Glastonbury (Richard only ever saw England as a way of financing his crusading ambitions). That said, Richard did put his nephew in charge of Glastonbury Abbey by making him the new abbot. Henry of Sully was only abbot of Glastonbury for three years or so; just long enough to oversee the discovery of King Arthur's grave and have Gerald of Wales write about it (see Gerald's statement on page 35). Richard's nephew then left Glastonbury as fast as he could,

'At this point, however, just when he seemed to be stabilizing his church's affairs, he was offered the see of Worcester and, as John of Glastonbury aptly put it, 'he fled like a hireling who sees the wolf approaching, exposing his sheep to the wolf's teeth.'
(James P. Carley, *Glastonbury Abbey*)

After the Great Fire of Glastonbury Abbey in 1184 very little was left standing above the ground. Two ancient 'pyramids' in the abbey graveyard towered above the ash and rubble. They would have been Saxon Crosses similar to the Bewcastle Cross shown here on the right; observe how the sides have decorative panels.

Gerald of Wales said that the 'pyramids' had writing upon them that implied that King Arthur was buried between them,

'there were certain indications in their writings that the body would be found there, and others in the letters engraven upon the pyramids, though they were much defaced by their extreme age'

but this is completely untrue. William of Malmesbury described the two 'pyramids', in detail, fifty years earlier (before Geoffrey of Monmouth's *History* about King Arthur) and there was nothing upon them to suggest the great hero; they were engraved with the names of early British and Saxon abbots of the abbey.

'CHAP. XXXII – Concerning the two pyramids.

I would willingly explain, if I could get at the truth, what those pyramids mean which, placed a few feet from the Old Church, border the Monks' Cemetery.

*The taller, which is nearest the church, has five tablets,
and is twenty-six feet high. This, though very old and
threatened with ruin, has not a few traces of antiquity,
which can be read though they cannot be fully understood.
In the top tablet, i.e., there is an image made to represent a
pontiff; in the second is an image representing royal
dignity, and the letters 'Her', 'Sexi', and 'Blisyer'; in the
third there are the names, 'Wemcrest', 'Bantomp',
'Winethegn'; in the fourth 'Bate', 'Wulfred', and 'Eanfled'; in
the fifth, which is also the bottom one, is an image and this
writing: 'Logwor, Weslicas, and Bregden, Swelwes,
Hwinganses, Bern'. The other pyramid is eighteen feet
high, and has four tablets in which this is to be read:
"Hedde bishop and Bregored, Beorward'. What these mean
I will not venture to define, but I conclude with some
hesitation that in the hollow stones the bones are contained
of those whose names are written outside. Certainly this
much can be asserted of Logwor, from whom Logweres-
beorh gets its name, which is now called Mons Acutus (the
pointed Mountain); Bregden, from which comes
Brentacnolle, now called Byen-tamerle. Beorwald was in
any case an abbot after Hemgiselus, concerning whom, and
all the rest who may come up, an orator will arise elsewhere
in a freer field.'*

(William of Malmesbury, *The Antiquities of Glastonbury*, 1135)

All of the above is quite dry and boring really isn't it? And
it is pretty much all that was left after the Great Fire. With
the sacred pilgrimage to St. David's long forgotten
Glastonbury was in need of being sexed-up a bit. It is
probable that the curiosity of the monks got the better of
them. The detail of the burial being within an hollowed-out
oak is interesting as the people of the Iron Age lake-villages
of Glastonbury used dug-out oak trees as canoes; but
Gerald of Wales describes Arthur's skeleton as that of a
giant with eye-sockets as wide as a palm-width. The
discovery of King Arthur's grave must be taken with a huge
pinch of salt; a most definite hoax, but one that has had far

reaching repercussions.

* **The motive**: There were many.

*'Tancred was understandably nervous about the crusaders but clearly he had nothing to fear from Philip's small force. His problem was Richard and the Angevin army. Although they were allies Richard's assault on Messina, and the circumstances in which the alliance had been forged, were hardly such as to dispel all of Tancred's doubts. Yet it was vital that he read Richard's intentions correctly. The King of Sicily's insecurity was fertile ground for Philip's diplomatic skill – these were just the kind of fears he had played upon when separating Henry II from his sons. What Philip wanted is clear enough: he wanted to save his sister's honour. She had now been betrothed to Richard for more than twenty years. To be cast aside after so long would be an intolerable insult. As the news came that Eleanor and Berengaria had crossed the Alps and were travelling southwards through Italy so Philip's concern grew. But at the same time their journey may have raised his hopes of drawing Tancred over to his side. For Tancred too had news which gave him cause for grave concern. Henry VI had left Germany and was heading in the direction of Sicily. It is not hard to imagine Tancred's feelings when he learned that Eleanor and Henry VI had met at Lodi, not far from Milan, on 20 January 1191. Just what lay behind this meeting? Were Richard and his old mother planning to throw in their lot with Henry? These were the fears which Richard had to dispel when he met Tancred at Catania and, eventually, he succeeded. The two Kings exchanged gifts as a token of their renewal of friendship. **Richard gave Tancred the sword Excalibur which had once belonged to King Arthur**. Tancred's gift was more prosaic, but possibly more useful: four large transport ships and fifteen galleys.'*

(John Gillingham, *Richard the Lionheart*)

The sword that Richard gave to King Tancred of Sicily must have been very valuable; worth the four large transport ships and fifteen galleys that Tancred gave in return; but more than this, Richard had also agreed that his heir would marry the daughter of Tancred. Richard's chosen heir was another of his nephews, Prince Arthur of Brittany... think about that for a moment.

Queen Eleanor of Aquitaine was married to Henry II,
she was mother of Richard the Lionheart and King John,
and she was grandmother of Prince Arthur of Brittany
and Henry of Sully the abbot of Glastonbury.
She and her daughter Marie of Champagne supported the writers
of the the Arthurian and Holy Grail romances.

That which was intended to happen was, after Richard the Lionheart had died, there would have been a new King Arthur of Britain. On marrying the daughter of the king of Sicily (as had already been arranged) he probably would have received the sword that was claimed to be Excalibur as part of his bride's dowry; but this return of Arthur never came to pass. Richard died sooner than expected in 1199 when Prince Arthur was about twelve years old. Richard's infamous younger brother took the throne and became King John. It is unknown for certain what became of Prince Arthur. John kept him as a prisoner and it was believed by most that he killed the young prince during a drunken rage in 1203; the prince would have been about sixteen years old.

The tomb of Richard the Lionheart
at Fontevraud Abbey, France.

Apart from the private Arthurian intrigues of the royal family of the Angevin Empire there were also secondary motives for the hoax of King Arthur's grave at Glastonbury; the first was political and spiritual, as it was designed to subdue the Welsh; the second was financial.

There is really no reason at all to trust Gerald of Wales' report that,

... it was above all King Henry II of England that most clearly informed the monks, as he had heard from an ancient Welsh bard, a singer of the past, that they would find the body at least sixteen feet beneath the earth, not in a tomb of stone, but in a hollow oak.'

Henry II died in 1189 so Gerald is actually putting words into a dead man's mouth; a useful dead man that gave the whole story a seal of royal approval and authority. Furthermore, the unnamed 'ancient Welsh bard' is no one in particular but he represents the bardic tradition that was very important to the Welsh people. Henry II, for the most part, had an antagonistic relationship with Wales and Richard I cared for it even less. Arthur was a rallying figure-head for Welsh uprisings (bards sang that one day he would return and reclaim the ancient lands of the Britons) and Richard wanted to be on crusade not skirmishing in his back yard. The discovery of Arthur's remains affirmed that he was truly dead and buried and not abiding in some sort of spiritual metaphysical other-world until his return.

Geoffrey of Monmouth had described Arthur being taken to the lady Morgen in her otherworldly isle. This was clearly questionable to the dogmatic Christian mindset of the 12th century; only Jesus and the Virgin Mary had *bodily risen*, or gone to some place *other* rather than be buried below the soil like the rest of humanity to await the day of judgement. Gerald of Wales was a devout religious man (he actually had ambitions on becoming bishop of St. David's); his jibe about Arthur resting in another world is clear to see,

*'Now the body of King Arthur, which **legend has feigned to have been transferred at his passing, as it were in ghostly form, by spirits to a distant place and to have been exempt from death**, was found in these our days at Glastonbury deep down in the earth...'*

Thus Arthur's grave at Glastonbury served to quell any Welsh uprisings (at least until Richard the Lionheart returned from the Holy Land) and it was also staged to deny any Welsh bardic songs of the Celtic otherworld; this would be a bit like saying to a Christian, 'we have proof that Jesus did not rise from the tomb because here is his skeleton.'

The Plantagenet kings of England, after kings Richard and John, continued to suppress the Welsh. The last true 'Prince of Wales' (Llewelyn II ap Gruffudd) was killed by Edward I in 1282; his severed head triumphantly placed on display in London. Edward I's son (later Edward II) was declared to be the new Prince of Wales and ever since then the title has been held by the eldest son of the English monarch whether they be Welsh or not – a complete theft of sovereignty that has lasted until the present day.

The final motive for the hoax of King Arthur's grave was of course financial. Henry II had died (and along with him his financial support) and King Richard didn't care at all. Glastonbury Abbey needed finance to continue rebuilding after the Great Fire. The popularity of King Arthur's grave worked (the Arthurian romances were very popular); in 1278 (four years before decapitating the last true Prince of Wales) Edward I and his queen visited Glastonbury to oversee King Arthur's remains being transferred to the high altar. In 1331 King Edward III and his queen visited Glastonbury too:

'ker-ching' the sound-effect of the abbey cash register.

The fame of Glastonbury being the place where King Arthur had been buried, and thus therefore that the Isle of Avalon was a real down-to-earth place rather than a mythic otherworld spirit realm, began to grow. Another version of the discovery of Arthur's grave was later written down at Margam Abbey in Wales. Although similar to the account by Gerald of Wales the *Margam Chronicle* is also very different (it is thought to date to around the mid 1200s),

'At Glastonbury the bones of the most famous Arthur, once King of Greater Britain, were found, hidden in a certain very ancient coffin. Two pyramids had been erected about them, in which certain letters were carved, but they could not be read because they were cut in a barbarous style and worn away. The bones were found on this occasion.

While they were digging a certain plot between the pyramids, in order to bury a certain monk who had begged and prayed the convent to be buried here, they found a certain coffin in which they saw a woman's bones with the hair still intact. When this was removed, they found another coffin below the first, containing a man's bones. This also being removed, they found a third below the first two, on which a lead cross was placed, on which was inscribed, "Here lies the famous king Arthur, buried in the Isle of Avalon." For that place was once surrounded by marshes, and is called the Isle of Avalon, that is "the isle of apples." For aval means, in British, an apple.

On opening the aforesaid coffin, they found the bones of the said prince, sturdy enough and large, which the monks transferred with suitable honour and much pomp into a marble tomb in their church. The first tomb was said to be that of Guinevere, wife of the same Arthur; the second, that of Mordred, his nephew; the third, that of the aforesaid prince.'

(From the *Chronicle of Margam Abbey, Annals of Margam*)

See the illustration on page 30. Gerald of Wales declared that King Arthur's grave was known about and looked for (because the 'ancient Welsh bard' told Henry II about it) but the *Margam Chronicle* states that the grave was discovered by accident due to the monks digging to bury one of their brethren who *'had begged and prayed the convent to be buried there'* (between the two stone 'pyramids'). Stranger too is that the *Margam Chronicle* describes three burials, one above the other, and that Mordred, Arthur's nephew, had been buried along with his uncle and aunt.

With the church-approved discovery of King Arthur's grave, and then the royal visits by King Edward I and his grandson, King Edward III, the pseudo-histories of Glastonbury became an established fact and also became a major influence upon the 13th century stories about the legend of the Holy Grail. Saint David gave the abbey a proto-Grail from Jerusalem (upon which the Lord had been sacrificed) and King Arthur's grave established Glastonbury as Avalon; a real world place no longer a mystical realm.

Joseph of Arimathea and the Holy Thorn
drawn by the author in 2011.

Depicts the Holy Thorn of Wearyall Hill that was hacked down by
vandals in 2010; it was planted there during the early 1950s.

The image of Joseph of Arimathea is from a stained-glass window
in St John's Church, Glastonbury; that was created in the 1930s.

Contrary to popular 'tradition' the legend of Joseph of Arimathea
is a 13th century invention of the monks of Glastonbury Abbey.

CHAPTER THREE
~ THE MYSTERIES OF THE HOLY GRAIL ~

Keeping it Simple

There are a great many different theories about the Holy Grail; what it was, is, and so on.

In recent decades, because of books like *The Holy Blood and the Holy Grail* inspiring popular works of fiction like Dan Brown's *The Davinci Code*, a popular idea is that the Grail is a metaphor for the blood descendants of Jesus and Mary Magdalene; which is an idea that falls apart very quickly under scrutiny.

When the Grail was first written about it was described as '*un Graal*', which is Old French for 'a Graal'. It was an enigmatic object, a thing of mystery, but it was not specifically 'Holy'. Later writers called it the *San Graal* (which is derived from *Sancta Graal*) meaning that it was sacred in a Christian context; that is, it had been sanctified by God, or the Church, in some way. Eventually *San Graal* became morphed into the single word, *Sangreal*, which by French mystics of the 19th century was cut in half to become 'Sang-Real'; which as a play on words can mean 'blood-royal' (from which evolved the popular conspiracy theory of the bloodline of Jesus) but the original descriptive '*un Graal*' cannot possibly have meant a royal blood-line.

12th century original spelling ~ **un Graal**
13th century sanctified spelling ~ **Sancta Graal**
13th century abbreviated spelling ~ **San Graal**
15th century it becomes one word ~ **Sangreal**
19th century it is split in to two words ~ **Sang Real**

The very first account of the Grail was given in *Perceval, Le Conte du* Graal; which was written by the French writer Chrétien de Troyes around 1190 AD. Chrétien never completed his story about the Grail and this open-ended intrigue tantalised his readers and inspired future generations of court poets and troubadours to complete his unfinished work with their own imaginations; which is why there are so many different (and contradictory) descriptions of the Grail. The most popular version (up until the modern blood-line of Jesus idea already discussed) was that the Grail was the Cup of the Last Supper, used by Joseph of Arimathea to gather Christ's blood during (or just after) the crucifixion; but even this was not the original Graal.

After Chrétien's unfinished story about the Graal a number of other writers picked up his project; there were four main ones and they are referred to as 'the first continuation', 'the second continuation' and so on but there is no conclusive evidence that any of these writers knew what conclusion Chrétien had in mind for his original story.

Around the same time as the 'Four Continuations' there was another writer, Robert de Boron, and he wrote a story called *Joseph D'Arimathe*. Boron introduced the popular back-story of the Grail being created by Joseph of Arimathea; and that the hallowed object was then protected by the Fisher Kings (which is a sacred blood-line legacy) but there is nothing in Chrétien's original story to imply any of Robert de Boron's invention.

In Chrétien's original story Sir Percival witnesses a mysterious procession of youths carrying sacred items,

The first youth carries a spear which drips blood.
Then two youths carry valuable silver candle-sticks.
Then a beautiful maiden carries, '*un Graal*'.

Percival failed to enquire what the purpose of this mysterious procession was; and his failure to question the meaning of the event meant that he failed in his quest and that the Fisher King's lands were doomed to remain a wasteland.

We have already seen (on page 15) that a 'graal' was a type of dish for serving food upon and this was the type of object that Chrétien de Troyes seems to of had in mind. Robert de Boron, in his story about Joseph of Arimathea, turned Chrétien's graal into the Cup of the Last Supper. Chrétien de Troyes stated that Sir Percival was a Welsh man and in the Welsh version of the story of Sir Percival, *Peredur*, the mysterious object is a decapitated head carried upon a blood-filled platter. A German version of the Percival story, *Parzival* describes the mysterious object as a special stone; which is assumed to have been the 'Philosopher's Stone' of the Alchemical tradition so,

Chrétien de Troyes ~ a deep serving dish.
Robert de Boron ~ the Cup of the Last Supper.
Peredur ~ a decapitated head upon a blood-filled platter.
Parzival ~ an alchemical stone.

Up until this stage the Grail story belonged to the adventures of Sir Percival (Peredur/Parsival) and to no other knight. Then came a series of stories that are collectively known as *The Vulgate Cycle.* It is in the Vulgate Cycle that Sir Percival gets pushed aside as the Grail knight and the honour and achievement is given to Sir Galahad the son of Sir Lancelot (although he is accompanied by Sir Percival, Sir Bors, and the maiden Dindraine). *The Vulgate Cycle* kept the Holy Grail variation of Robert de Boron (the Cup of the Last Supper) and from then onwards the decapitated head of *Peredur* and the alchemical stone of *Parzival* were dropped in favour of the Christian chalice.

*T*he *Vulgate Cycle* evolved into the *Post Vulgate Cycle*, which inspired Sir Thomas Mallory's *Le Morte D'Arthur;* which was the primary version that inspired Victorian romantics like Alfred, Lord Tennyson and the Pre-Raphaelite Brotherhood; who then created the most popular versions of the stories in the modern world. Thus most people think of the Holy Grail as the Cup of the Last Supper within which Joseph of Arimathea gathered Christ's blood but this was not Chrétien de Troyes' original 'graal'.

The Grail and other sacred hallows of 'The Mysteries'

Along with the ever-present blood-dripping spear, the Graal is just one of many sacred and mystical items (known as 'hallows') to be found in the weird and surreal world of Arthurian romance. For instance, as much as it is Sir Percival's destiny to seek the Graal, in a romance known as *The High History of the Holy Graal* Sir Gawain has to find the 'Saracen's Sword' that decapitated John the Baptist (which of course brings to mind the head dripping in blood in the Welsh story *Peredur*). The realms of Arthurian romance are deliberately strange and it is a mistake to ride through their forests looking for true history; they are mystical stories drawn from Mystery Tradition imagery.

The Mystery Traditions were the spiritual teachings of the pre-Christian world. The most famous of which were the Eleusinian Mysteries but there were many others like those of Isis, Mithras, and so on. Christianity itself was formed from elements of the many pagan Mystery schools of the Roman Empire. The Mysteries used theatre, stories, symbolic objects, and sacred artefacts, to explain many esoteric spiritual truths and wisdom. The Arthurian romances are actually a western European collection of older, mostly Celtic, wisdom stories retold in a medieval Christian context. The Arthurian Mysteries are many, and varied, and they deserve an entire book of discussion in their own right; maybe one day.

Mystery Rites and ritual teachings were usually performed in darkened rooms (or even caves) with torches or candles used to illuminate sacred icons or to reveal meaningful 'enlightenments'; thus in the first written account about the story of the Graal, Chrétien de Troyes also described youths carrying candlesticks behind the spear that was dripping blood. The main character in the story of the Graal, Sir Percival, is a stereotypical Fool bumbling his way through the adventure; as he learns things so too does the reader (or audience of the Mystery Play). Sir Percival failed in his quest because he did not ask what the procession of the Graal was for. Quite simply, Mysteries cannot be revealed until a participant first asks 'why?' because an unquestioning mind learns nothing. This is very different to organised religions in which followers have blind faith and question nothing; following as sheep do a shepherd.

In the 12th to 14th centuries asking 'why?' was dangerously heretical. The word 'heresy' simply means 'to choose' and a heretic was one who chose to think differently to official doctrine; the Catholic Church terminated heretics like the Cathars, and Knights Templars accused of heresy were tortured and burnt at the stake. It was probably the scent of the pagan Mystery Traditions behind the story of the Graal that motivated the devout Christian, Robert de Boron, to create the whole Joseph of Arimathea, Cup of the Last Supper, back-story to Chrétien's unfinished Graal saga (and yet, ironically, a vessel used for collecting blood from a sacrifice upon a cross was also a pagan Mystery Tradition image; as will be explained).

Robert de Boron's Christianised version of Chrétien's Graal should be approached with extreme caution; he was a 'hell and brimstone' fanatic. His *Joseph D'Arimathe* begins with the lines,

"ALL SINFUL PEOPLE should know this: that before Our Lord came to Earth, He made the prophets speak His name and announce His coming to the world. At the time of which I speak all people went to Hell - even the prophets..."

And his story unfolds with the same constant religious zeal and angst. Robert de Boron is unpleasantly anti-Semitic in his story and he blames the Jews for the crucifixion of Jesus rather than the Romans (a common Christian opinion of his era). The main point that I am trying to make is that whilst the Joseph of Arimathea legend of the Holy Grail is the most popular it is actually a fanatical Christian corruption of Chrétien de Troyes' mysterious Graal. To approach understanding the original Mystery we have to go back to something older (something that Robert de Boron was attempting to convert, cover-up, and rewrite).

Chrétien's mystical objects were the spear dripping with blood, illuminated by candlesticks, followed by the Graal; but in the world of Arthurian romance there are many other mystical and magical artefacts (like Arthur's sword, Excalibur) and there is even a tradition of Merlin and the Thirteen Treasures of Britain (none of which were a Graal). Arthurian romance actually encoded Jesus as the Winter King (wounded by a **spear**, with his blood caught in a cup/**bowl**) and John the Baptist as the Summer King (decapitated by a **sword** and his head upon a dish/**platter**); I'll go into this in more detail in Appendix II. These four sacred items are a medieval Christian adaptation of four Celtic treasures of divine sovereignty that are remembered in Ireland as the **Spear** of Lugh, the **Sword** of Nuada, the **Cauldron** of the Dagda, and the **Stone** of Destiny.

The Round Table and Star-Lore of the Mysteries

The permanent mural of the Mystery Traditions, eternal in the heavens as if painted by the gods themselves, are the stars and fixed constellations of the night sky. Unlike manuscripts, paintings, and statues, that which is written in the heavens cannot be burnt, destroyed, or erased. The heavenly constellations are thus seemingly immortal and never-changing; at least during the span of a human life time. Furthermore, because of Earth's annual orbit around the Sun, the stars repeat the same story every year; creating an endless wisdom of cycles and renewal. The star-lore intrigues of Arthurian romance are made blatantly apparent in the accounts of one of Arthur's most iconic symbols; the Round Table.

The Round Table is described in *La Queste del Saint Graal* as such,

"... The Round Table was constructed, not without great significance, upon the advice of Merlin. By its name the Round Table is meant to signify the round world and the round canopy of the planets and the elements in the firmament, where are to be seen the stars and many other things..."

And in *The High History of the Holy Graal* it is stated that three-hundred and sixty-six knights sat at the Round Table; which means it had a seat for each day of the year (you need three-hundred and sixty-six seats because three-hundred and sixty-five is not a complete year, it is a quarter-day short of a year). A year is defined by the Sun's apparent journey through the twelve signs of the zodiac and the zodiac was the celestial story-book of the ancient Mystery Traditions.

The zodiac was always of great significance and even though the Church forbid the study of astrology the signs of the zodiac still adorn many cathedrals and churches. The wonderful ornate entrance to the abbey of Vèzelay depicts Jesus surrounded by the signs of the zodiac (see opposite page) and the most important cathedral of England, Canterbury, still has medieval roundels of the signs of the zodiac upon the floor of its high altar. Quite simply the signs of the zodiac represent the heavenly realm. However, the zodiac also had many deeper meanings and it was used to represent the spiritual reality within each individual as well as representing the divine map of the soul's journey after death. Learning the spiritual nature of one's inner self was what the Mystery Traditions were all about and the stars were the voice of guidance from the heavenly kingdom itself; shining down upon mortals since the very beginning.

The ornate zodiacal entrance to the
Abbaye Sainte-Marie-Madeleine de Vézelay
in the Avallonnais, Burgundy, France.

Note the lights upon the floor of the central aisle which is a deliberate phenomena created by the Sun at Summer Solstice.

The great pilgrimage from Vézelay to Cape Finisterre on the west coast of Spain (see map on page 19), the Camino de Santiago de Compostela, represents the heavenly spirit-path of the Milky Way (Compostela means 'field of stars'). Furthermore the old name for the hill of Vézelay is Scorpion Hill and the Milky Way crosses the night sky from the cusp of Taurus/Gemini to the cusp of Sagittarius/Scorpio. Is this a coincidence? A straight line drawn from Vézelay (Scorpion Hill) through Bourges (the heart-centre of France) aligns directly with Cape Finisterre, the final destination of the Camino de Santiago de Compostela. All of which is but an example of just how deeply zodiacal lore permeated through medieval French culture (and into the Arthurian romances as well). The next chapter explores Vézelay in much greater detail but for now here is the star-lore of the Holy Grail.

The Heavenly Grail

The entire night sky can be seen as a vast circular ocean of stars. For the ancient Mystery Traditions and the Arthurian Mysteries we are looking at the stars of the northern hemisphere (the southern hemisphere has different constellations). In very ancient times, thousands of years ago, the night sky was divided by an imaginal grid of twelve equal sections; each named after a constellation that the Sun visits during its cyclic perambulation through the stars each year. These twelve sections of the night sky are called the 'signs' of the zodiac and are not to be confused with the 'constellations' of the zodiac. Each of the twelve sections of the night sky contain many other constellations, not just those of the zodiac. For instance, in the Virgo area of the night sky there is also the constellation of Corvus the Crow and in the Gemini section there is Orion the Hunter. In the Leo area of the heavens is the constellation of Crater the Cup (or wine-mixing bowl); the 'Heavenly Grail' of the ancient Mystery Traditions.

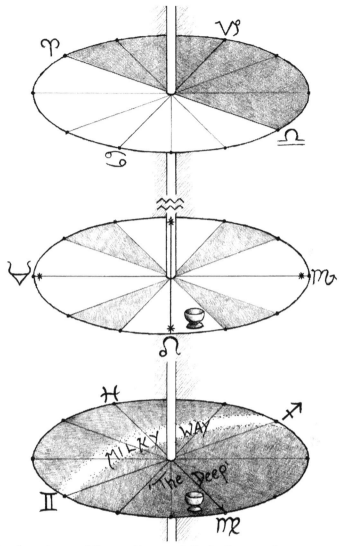

The twelve signs of the zodiac and their three primary patterns.

Top; **The Sun Cross** ~ formed by the two Solstices and Equinoxes.

Middle; **The Royal Star Cross** ~ Crater the 'Heavenly Grail' sits at the foot of this cross within the sign of Leo the Lion.

Bottom; **The Milky Way spirit-path** ~ Crater is also the Celtic Cauldron of renewal in the deep depths of the Other-world.

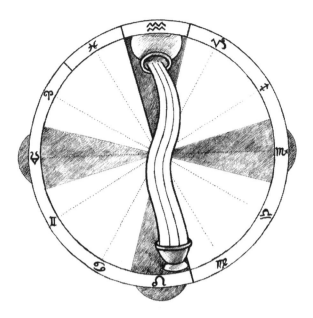

The Royal Star Cross with the ever-flowing waters of Aquarius pouring into Crater at the foot of the cross in the sign of Leo.

A Mithraic Tauroctony; depicts Crater as a wine-mixing vessel beside a lion for Leo in position to receive the sacrificial blood.

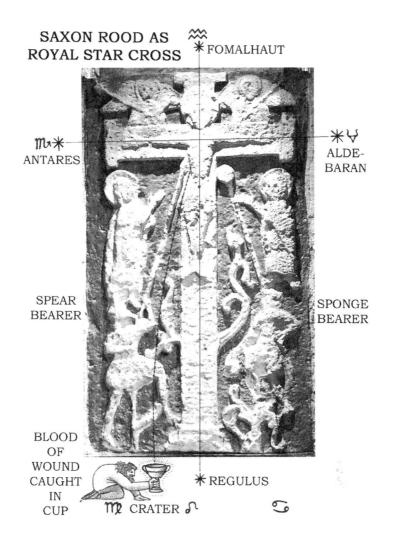

SAXON ROOD AS ROYAL STAR CROSS

♒ ✳FOMALHAUT

♏✳ ANTARES

✳♉ ALDE-BARAN

SPEAR BEARER

SPONGE BEARER

BLOOD OF WOUND CAUGHT IN CUP

✳ REGULUS

♍ CRATER ♌

♋

The Royal Star Cross as the crucifixion.

The legend of Joseph of Arimathea collecting the blood of Christ
(Robert de Boron's version of the Graal)
is star-lore from the pre-Christian pagan Mystery Traditions.

The images on these two pages illustrate how Crater (the 'Heavenly Grail') relates to the foot of the cross (the Royal Star Cross) and shows how it was used in Mithraic symbolism to catch sacrificial blood many centuries before Robert de Boron wrote his version of the story of the Graal.

Each sign of the zodiac governs a part of the body and Leo governs the heart; so therefore Crater, the Heavenly Grail, sits within the heart of all people. This Mystery teaching relates to ideas about the internal alchemy of the spiritual-energy at the centre of every living being and it is known as the Middle Bowl, Middle Cauldron, Middle Dantien, or Tiphareth of the 'heavenly man' (zodiacal man) of the Cabbalistic Tree of Life; here we have many layers of complexity but a universal Mystery teaching common to many cultures.

Bringing it back to Glastonbury

Robert de Boron's Cup of the Last Supper soon became the most popular version of the Grail story and this made the legend of Joseph of Arimathea popular too. Robert de Boron wrote his *Joseph D'Arimathe* some time in the early 1200s. Shortly afterwards, some time around 1220, an anonymous writer wrote a Grail romance in French, *Perlesvaus* (another variation of Sir Percival). In the late Victorian era *Perlesvaus* was translated into English by Sebastian Evans and he retitled it *The High History of the Holy Graal.* The '*High History*' is unique amongst all of the other Grail romances in that it claims to be based upon a Latin history that was kept at Glastonbury Abbey; in its final pages it states that,

*'The **Latin** from whence this **history** was drawn into Romance was taken in the **Isle of Avalon**, in the holy house of religion that standeth at the head of the Moors Adventurous, **there where King Arthur and Queen Guenievre lie**, according to the witness of the good men religious that are therein, that have the whole history thereof, true from the beginning even to the end.'*

THE·HIGH·HISTORY·
OF·THE·HOLY·GRAAL·

Whilst the *High History* quote does not state 'Glastonbury' no other place claims to be the burial place of Arthur and Guinevere. The quote from the *High History* is interesting for a couple of reasons. Firstly, that at least by the year 1220 (or there abouts) Glastonbury Abbey was believed to hold the true history of the Grail (*'true from the beginning even to the end'*) and secondly, that Glastonbury

Abbey itself was actually situated within one of the geographical locations of the Grail story (*'at the head of the Moors Adventurous'*) which meant that the Grail saga corresponded with the abbey's immediate landscape. At the risk of being overly repetitive let me remind you that the proto-Grail of Saint David's Sapphire Alter (from Jerusalem and upon which the Lord had been sacrificed) was kept at Glastonbury as a sacred relic and was celebrated by many pilgrims less than a century before *Perlesvaus* was written; and that a neighbouring castle, less than a day's horse-ride away, belonged to the Perceval family. Glastonbury had all of this long before it acquired Robert de Boron's Joseph of Arimathea 'tradition'.

'Jo of A' and the 'spurious' history of Glastonbury

In 1129 abbot Henry of Blois, having recently discovered the Sapphire Altar of Saint David, had William of Malmesbury write the history of Glastonbury to promote the sacred treasure that David had brought back from Jerusalem. In his *Antiquities of Glastonbury*, which he completed in 1135, William made no mention of Joseph of Arimathea at all. About one-hundred years later, circa 1240, an unknown person added the Joseph of Arimathea tradition into the *Antiquities of Glastonbury*.

1135 ~ William of Malmesbury completes his *Antiquities of Glastonbury*; he makes no mention of Joseph of Arimathea.
1200-1210 ~ Robert de Boron's *Joseph D'Arimathe* introduces Joseph of Arimathea into the Holy Grail legend.
1220 (circa) ~ *The High History of the Holy Graal* includes Joseph of Arimathea and claims that the true history of the Graal was kept at Glastonbury Abbey.
1240 (circa) ~ an unknown hand adds the Joseph of Arimathea tradition into the *Antiquities of Glastonbury*.

There is a modern English translation of the *Antiquities*

of Glastonbury (which was originally written in Latin). The English version was translated in 1908 by Frank Lomax; and he explains in his introduction that the *Antiquities* contains many interpolations that were added long after William of Malmesbury had died. Most importantly there are entire sections that claim to come from the *'Charter of the Blessed Patrick'*. Frank Lomax clearly states that this interpolated manuscript is known to be 'spurious'. This spurious *Charter* is the source of Glastonbury's entire Arimathean tradition. In short, as with King Arthur's grave, the Joseph of Arimathea tradition is yet another hoax of Glastonbury Abbey; yet again attempting to cash-in on the growing popularity of the Arthurian romances.

Like a ridiculous Monty Python sketch, one interpolation into the *Antiquities of Glastonbury* describes Saint David visiting Glastonbury in order to build a church; but audaciously declares that whilst he was on his way to Glastonbury David had a dream in which Jesus himself told him that he needn't bother as a church already existed there established by he himself (Jesus). In compensation for his wasted journey Saint David is allowed to build a second smaller church next to the old church that Jesus dedicated. You cannot make this stuff up (well, actually you can, and the monks of Glastonbury Abbey did),

'CHAP. XV – Of St. David, the Archbishop.

How highly this spot was esteemed in those days that great man David, Archbishop of St. David's, has testified, more than need be illustrated by our relation. He learnt of the antiquity and sanctity of the church by a Divine oracle. Being therefore bent on dedicating it, he came up to the spot accompanied by seven bishops, of whom he was primate. When everything had been made ready which the customary dedication service demanded, night beginning to wear away, as he thought, he was indulging himself with slumber on the festival. When, therefore, all their senses were lapped into sleep, he saw the Lord Jesus standing by his side demanding in gentle tones why they had come. And when he promptly explained why, the Lord recalled him to his senses with these words:

"The church had been dedicated long ago by Himself in honour of His Mother, and it was not seemly that it should be re-dedicated by human hands."

Even as He spoke He was seen to make a hole in the palm of his hand with His finger, and He added this:
"Let him take that for a sign that he might not repeat what Himself had done before-hand. But because his intention had not been so much a bold as a devout one, his punishment should not be prolonged. Finally, on the following morning, when he (St. David) was going to say the words in the Mass through Him and with Him and in Him, the full strength of salvation should flow back to him."
The primate, shaken out of his slumber by these terrors, just as he was then pallid from an ulcerous sore, so afterwards he hailed the prophecy as true; but lest they should seem to have come out for naught, he immediately set about building and dedicating another church.'
(Antiquities of Glastonbury)

The above quote is clearly an attempt to absorb the earlier history of Glastonbury Abbey (being established by Saint David) with the spurious Arimathean tradition declared by the *Charter of the Blessed Patrick*. This quote is not historical evidence; it is the writing of an unknown thirteenth-century person declaring that Saint David dreamt of Jesus saying 'don't dedicate the church in Glastonbury because I have already done so'.

The *Charter's* spurious history begins within an account of the Apostle, St. Philip, sending twelve of his disciples to Britain to preach the good faith; the leader of the twelve was Philip's 'dearest friend', Joseph of Arimathea, 'who buried the Lord'. The *Charter* states that Joseph of Arimathea came to Glastonbury in the year 63 AD (and this date is important as I'll explain). This is the only mention of Joseph of Arimathea in the entire *Antiquities of Glastonbury*, and there is no mention of the Holy Grail. An unnamed 'barbaric king' gives Joseph of Arimathea and his companions twelve hides of land to live upon (one hide per person). After which, in 64 AD, a vision of the angel Gabriel tells them to build a church in honour of the Virgin Mary and,

'... as it was the first church in the kingdom (Britain) God's Son distinguished it with greater dignity by dedicating it in honour of his Mother.'
(*Antiquities of Glastonbury*)

Then, following this grand beginning in which Britain's very first church was sanctified by Jesus himself,

'The said saints continued to live in the same hermitage for many years, and were at last liberated from the prison of the flesh. The place then began to be a covert for wild beasts.'
(*Antiquities of Glastonbury*)

It is an interesting observation that the 'first church in the kingdom', dedicated by Jesus himself, had such an ineffective impression upon the locals that it was allowed to fall into neglect; becoming 'a covert for wild beasts'. The spurious *Charter of the Blessed Patrick* then tells how a century later (166 AD) a certain King Lucius sent a request to Pope Eleutherius to send missionaries to Christianise the Britons. The Pope sent saints Phagan and Deruvian who eventually found the old church that had been established in the Isle of Avalon by Joseph of Arimathea and his followers. None of which could possibly have happened because in 166 AD Britain was a dynamic part of the Roman Empire; there was no 'King Lucius' and Christians were not tolerated by Rome until the 4th century.

'By the fourteenth century the monks themselves had a tradition concerning their earliest volume: in St Patrick's Charter (itself a thirteenth-century forgery) it is narrated that in an old oratory on the top of the Tor St Patrick found a badly damaged volume containing the Acts of the Apostles and the gesta (that is acts and deeds) of St Phagan and St Deruvian, a volume presumably dating from the second century when the missionaries described by William of Malmesbury arrived at Glastonbury. Needless to say, no book remotely answering this description appears in surviving records.'
(James P. Carley, *Glastonbury Abbey*)

'William of Malmesbury's treatise on the Antiquities of Glastonbury (c.1125) was interpolated a century after his death with a fictitious chapter which described Philip the Apostle preaching the Gospel in Gaul together with Joseph of Arimathea, whom he sent to England with twelve disciples.'
(*The Oxford Dictionary of Saints*)

The actual history of Glastonbury is this: that every single archaeological dig done in and around Glastonbury has revealed the evidence of Roman occupation; there is even evidence that there was a pagan Roman temple on top of Glastonbury Tor (although this is very rarely promoted and certainly not by the Tor visitor information boards).

Rome invaded Britain in 43 AD and within the first four years it completely conquered the south of the country; which included the territory of Glastonbury and the Somerset Levels. The notion that any 'barbaric king' in 63 AD could have granted Joseph of Arimathea and followers land of their own is absurd; especially the claim that the following year they built the first church in the land as this same year (64 AD) was also the year of the Great Fire of

Rome. Christians became public enemy number one after the Great Fire and Rome stamped down upon them with the most vicious forms of brutality – they were regularly burnt to death and thrown to lions for entertainment. Quite simply, any Roman authority in the Glastonbury area would never allow a Christian community to build a church.

The West Country was a war-zone at this time. Just two years before Joseph of Arimathea is said to have arrived the great Celtic warrior queen, Boudica, had almost succeeded in defeating the Roman occupation of Britain. In 64 AD the legionaries marching through the land were still on guard and anticipating threats from every direction; a major concern were the Silures (a Celtic tribe from South Wales) who were not defeated until the Romans established the fort of Caerleon in 74 AD. Even the claim that the saints Phagan and Deruvian established a Christian community in Glastonbury in 166 AD is equally absurd for all of the same reasons. Britain's earliest saint, Saint Alban, was killed for being a Christian as late as 300 AD and Somerset had many pagan Roman temples that were still active in the 4th century. Ironically, a deity that was popular with the Roman legionaries, Mithras, was often depicted letting sacrificial blood flow into a Crater, the 'Heavenly Grail', (see page 60) and there was a Mithraeum in Caerleon. So, the many classical Mystery Traditions were an influence upon the Romano-British Dark Age culture of Somerset (during the Age of Arthur) as the many Roman mosaics of the West Country clearly define.

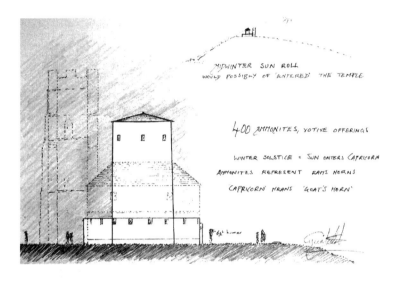

An artistic impression of the Romano-British temple on the summit of Glastonbury Tor; based upon archaeological evidence in the Somerset Archives, Taunton. The evidence is of a circular temple on the east side of the current tower; the height of the temple can only be guessed. Roman temples had a central primary shrine dedicated to one specific deity (like Mars, Apollo, Mercury, or Minerva) around which were smaller shrines for other gods and goddesses. It most likely had a mosaic floor and murals and it probably also functioned as a fire beacon for communicating with surrounding and distant hill tops – the Tor being the most prominent hill of the Somerset Levels.
This pagan temple of Light existed in Glastonbury long before any Christian church was established.

Quite obviously, the main purpose for the 13th century story of Joseph of Arimathea coming to Glastonbury was for the abbey to establish an, as ancient as possible, claim to the Twelve Hides of Glastonbury; a rather large and valuable territory of Glastonbury Abbey that remained tax-free for centuries because of this spurious history.

'Within its precinct the Benedictine life flourished – the liturgy, the works of education and charity, the crafts and music, the development of the library. Outside, the ancient 'Twelve Hides' of land were enlarged by bequests, donations and purchases, till the saying went that if the Abbot of Glastonbury married the Abbess of Shaftesbury, they would have more land than the King of England.'
(Geoffrey Ashe, *Avalonian Aeon*)

- 'Ker-ching' the sound-effect of the abbey cash register.

Abbot John Chinnock (who was abbot of Glastonbury between 1375 and 1420) promoted the 'tradition' of Joseph of Arimathea for all it was worth,

'In the 1340s Edward III contemplated founding an order based on the Round Table and became keenly interested in Glastonbury's version of the Arthurian/Joseph of Arimathea legend as promoted by John of Glastonbury. Later, when Edward lost enthusiasm for the project Walter de Monington decided to let the Joseph story fall back into obscurity. In Chinnock's abbacy two factors made the Joseph legend suddenly much more relevant. One of the results of the Great Schism was the development of the Conciliar movement; theorists now argued that councils were superior to the pope in some areas and that precedence in councils should be determined by the dates of foundation of the various national churches. If Joseph of Arimathea did establish a church at Glastonbury, then Glastonbury (and England itself) ranked among the most senior churches. Combined with this national issue was the local question of supplement of income. If more money could not be generated from the estates, then there was

still the possibility of encouraging a larger volume of pilgrims, which Joseph's fame as a Glastonbury saint would certainly do. It is not surprising, then, that shortly after he became abbot, Chinnock commissioned a new copy of John's chronicle – containing a fully developed account of Joseph's mission to Glastonbury and his building of the wattled Old Church – to be written. In 1382, moreover, Chinnock restored a small ruined chapel in the cemetery and had it rededicated to St Michael and St Joseph of Arimathea. Conspicuous in its decorations was a life-size triptych featuring Joseph's role in the Deposition. Not much later, Chinnock caused a large manuscript (3ft 8 in x 21 ¼ in) containing John's account of King Arthur, St Patrick, the translation of St Dunstan, the story of St Joseph's mission and various other excerpts to be written in an elegant book hand. It was mounted on a folding frame and was set up in a conspicuous place in the church where it could be read by visitors.

There are no written statistics to indicate how many new pilgrims were attracted, but a variety of other indications show that the legend 'caught on'. As a result of the Joseph association Chinnock quickly managed to win primacy among abbots at a national synod; later the English Church demanded and obtained parity with other apostolic churches at the councils of Pisa (1409), Constance (1417), Siena (1424) and Basel (1434).'

(James P. Carley, *Glastonbury Abbey*)

Which isn't a bad result for a spurious story invented in the 13th century.

* * *

The contradictions between the two Josephs of Arimathea.

There are two Joseph of Arimathea stories (or 'traditions') and they contradict each other. There is Robert de Boron's Joseph of Holy Grail fame and there is Glastonbury Abbey's Joseph of the Twelve Hides (and no Grail); here are the contradictions.

Glastonbury ~ Glastonbury's original Jo of A tradition is actually very minimal but it became massively embellished by later generations. The original claims were simply,

1 ~ Joseph of Arimathea arrived in 63 AD.
2 ~ He and his followers were given Twelve Hides of land.
3 ~ They built the first church (and somehow it was dedicated by Jesus himself).
4 ~ Jo of A and his followers lived out their years and then died in Glastonbury.

And that is it. There is no mention of anything resembling the Holy Grail.

Robert de Boron ~ Robert de Boron was the very first writer to equate Joseph of Arimathea with the Holy Grail; he wrote the first story about Joseph of Arimathea; and his version pre-dates Glastonbury's 'spurious' tradition by a few decades; one can thus assume that he is the authority on Joseph of Arimathea and the Holy Grail and as such it would be wise to look at what he actually did say,

1 ~ He never mentions Glastonbury at all.
2 ~ He describes the Grail as being taken to the 'vales of Avaron' not the 'isle of Avalon'.
3 ~ He specifically states that Jo of A ended his days in the land and country of his birth; that is he died in Arimathea not Britain.
4 ~ He describes Bron (Jo of A's brother-in-law) as being the first Fisher King and that he and his descendants took the Grail to the 'Occident' (the west) on Jo of A's bequest. Sir Percival is descended from this Fisher King bloodline (the hereditary custodians of the Grail; as is his sister Dindraine).
5 ~ He describes Christianity as being **new** to Britain in the 5th century (during the time of King Vortigern and Merlin).

The Glastonbury Joseph of Arimathea tradition and Robert de Boron's original account of Joseph of Arimathea do not tell the same story; and the Glastonbury account is known to be spurious.

'... So departed the rich Fisher King – of whom many words have since been spoken – while Joseph stayed behind and ended his days in the land and country of his birth.'
(Robert de Boron)

One has to make a choice: one either has Joseph of Arimathea in Glastonbury in the 1st century and no Holy Grail, just twelve hides of land; or, one has Joseph of Arimathea and the Holy Grail but not in Glastonbury. One cannot have it both ways (although by later centuries Glastonbury would claim it all and add more cream to the cake with the legend of the Holy Thorn and Jesus himself visiting Glastonbury as a child with his uncle Joe).

Before we get too tangled up with the contradictory intrigues of Joseph of Arimathea and the Holy Grail we can simply dismiss it all. Now is a good time to remind ourselves that actually the original story of the Holy Grail was that of the mysterious 'Graal' (the serving dish) described by Chrétien de Troyes; it was never Jo of A's Cup of the Last Supper anyway. Back to Chretien de Troyes, the original writer about the Graal.

Chrétien's Connections

On page 55 I introduced the four Celtic treasures of divine sovereignty; the Sword of Nuada, the Spear of Lugh, the Cauldron of the Dagda, and the Stone of Destiny. These four items are the original Gaelic version of the sacred hallows of the Celtic Mysteries; the Mystery teachings of the Celtic west. In the medieval Christian mysticism of the Arthurian Grail romances the four treasures were absorbed as the sword that decapitated John the Baptist and the platter upon which his head was served to King Herod; and the spear that pierced Jesus during his crucifixion and the bowl, (vessel, cup, or cruets), that were used to collect his blood. Chrétien actually described all four treasures in his story of Sir Percival (which is an important observation that is usually overlooked); here is the full quote (It begins with the rich Fisher King giving Percival a very special sword),

'While they talked, a young attendant entered at the door, a **sword** hanging by his neck. He handed it to the wealthy man. The latter, drawing it out halfway, clearly saw where it had been made, this being engraved on the blade. He also noticed that it was made of such fine steel that it could not break into pieces except by a singular peril known only to the man who had forged it. The attendant who brought it spoke. "Sir, the blonde maiden, your niece who is so beautiful, sends you this gift. You have never seen so noble a sword of its length and width. Bestow it on whomever you please. But my lady would be most happy if it were given to one who would use it well. The man who forged the sword made only three, and since he is about to die, he can never again forge another **sword** like this one."

The lord [the Fisher King] invested the young stranger [Percival] with the **sword**, holding it by the rings, which were worth a treasure. The **sword**'s hilt was of the finest gold of Arabia or of Greece, the scabbard of gold brocade from Venice. The **sword**, thus richly decked, the lord presented to the youth. "Dear sir, this **sword** was appointed and destined for you. And I wish you to have it. Buckle it on and test it," he said.

The youth thanked him for it and buckled it on, not fastening it too tight. He then unsheathed the naked blade and, after holding it a little, put it back into its scabbard.

You can be certain that it greatly suited him at his side and, even more, in his grasp. In time of need, it surely seemed, he would use it as a nobleman might.

*Behind him, around the brightly blazing fire, he noticed a knight bachelor, and recognised him as the one guarding his armour. He entrusted him with his **sword**, and the knight kept it for him. The youth then took his seat again at the side of the lord, who showed him great honour. And about them was light as bright as candles may furnish in a hall.*

*While they talked of this and that, a young attendant entered the room, holding **a shining lance** by the middle of its shaft. He passed between the fire and those seated on the bed, and all present saw **the shining lance** with its shining head. A drop of blood fell from the tip of **the lance**, and that crimson drop ran all the way down to the attendant's hand. The youth who had come there that night beheld this marvel and refrained from asking how this could be. He remembered the warning of the man who had made him a knight, he who had instructed and taught him to guard against speaking too much. The youth feared that if he asked a question, he would be taken for a peasant. He therefore asked nothing.*

*Two more attendants then entered, bearing in their hands candelabra of fine gold inlaid with niello. Handsome indeed were the attendants carrying the candelabra. On each candelabrum ten candles, at the very least, were burning. Accompanying the attendants was a beautiful, gracious, and elegantly attired young lady holding between her two hands **a bowl** ['un graal']. When she entered holding this **serving bowl**, such brilliant illumination appeared that the candles lost their brightness just as the stars and the moon do with the appearance of the sun. Following her was another young lady holding a **silver carving platter**. The **bowl**, which came first, was of fine pure gold, adorned with* *many kinds of precious jewels, the richest and most costly found on sea or land, those on the bowl undoubtedly more valuable than any others. Exactly as the **lance** had done, the **bowl** and the **platter** passed in front of the bed and went from one room into another.*

*The youth watched them pass and dared not ask who was served from the **bowl**, for always he took to heart the words of the wise and worthy man. I fear harm may result, for I have often heard it said that there are times when too much silence is the same as too much speech. Whether for good or ill, he did not ask them any question.'*
(Chrétien de Troyes, *Le Conte du Graal*, translation by David Staines)

Whilst the Graal is the most radiant and important of all of the sacred items (and it would correspond with the Cauldron of the Dagda) Sir Percival failed to ask anything about any of the treasures; not even the magnificent sword that he is generously given. He just talks about 'this and that' and thus he fails the test of the Graal. The rest of his adventure is about how he learns to understand his error and attempts to make amends. However, Chrétien never finished writing his story and so the reader, the audience, and the whole world, have been left with an unexplained enigma that has shone down to us through the centuries.

Very little is known about Chrétien de Troyes himself. He presumably came from Troyes, in France, or he at least spent a significant amount of time there. It is guessed that he was born some time in the 1130s. He dedicated one of his earliest stories to Marie the Countess of Champagne. Marie became the Countess in 1159 when she married Henry the Liberal; so Chrétien's dedication has to correspond with this year or afterwards. His unfinished story about the Graal, he dedicated to Count Philip of Flanders. Philip became the Count of Flanders in 1168 and set off on the Third Crusade in 1190; and then died in the

Holy Land in 1191. So Chrétien's *Le conte du Graal* had to have been started before 1191. Count Philip was in Sicily with Richard the Lionheart when Excalibur was gifted to King Tancred; it is possible that Chrétien was also present in the crusading entourage of Count Philip. It has been speculated that Chrétien died on crusade, along-side Count Philip, and that this is why he never completed *Le conte du Graal* but nobody knows for sure. Count Philip of Flanders actually commissioned Chrétien to write the story about the Graal, Chrétien says so himself,

*'Therefore Chrétien's labour will not be wasted when, **at the count's command**, he endeavours and strives to put into rhyme the finest tale that may be told at a royal court. This is the Story of the Graal, **from the book the count gave him**...'*

(Chrétien de Troyes, *Le conte du Graal*)

So let us pause and digest: in 1191 King Richard the Lionheart gave the sword Excalibur as a gift to King Tancred of Sicily. This same year Richard's nephew, Henry of Sully, the abbot of Glastonbury, oversaw the 'discovery' of King Arthur's Grave at Glastonbury Abbey. Richard's chosen heir was another of his nephews, Prince Arthur of Brittany, who was thus destined to become the new King Arthur of England (and the entire Angevin Empire) and acquire Excalibur when he married Tancred's daughter, the princess of Sicily. Furthermore in Sicily, along-side King Richard, was Philip the Count of Flanders, the very man that gave the source material for the story of the Graal to Chrétien de Troyes to turn into Arthurian Romance. What are the chances of that?

We have a tight-knit family intrigue here. Chrétien de Troyes wrote for Marie of Champagne and Philip of Flanders; they were cousins and close friends. More importantly, Marie was the eldest daughter of Eleanor of Aquitaine which made her Richard the Lionheart's half sister (her father was the King of France, Richard's the King of England). Eleanor of Aquitaine had first been married to King Louis VII of France and then married Henry II of England. Both Eleanor of Aquitaine and her daughter Marie of Champagne were enthusiastic patrons of the writers of Arthurian Romance.

Morgan le Fay
And the Faerie Magic of the Celtic West

In one of his earliest stories (*Erec and Enide*) Chrétien de Troyes refers to the Isle of Avalon whilst describing the lords and nobles that attended the wedding of Erec and Enide,

> '... Greslemuef of **Finisterre** brought twenty companions. And his brother Guinguemar came too, who was Lord of the **Isle of Avalon**. We have heard it said of him that he was a lover of Morgan le Fay, and that had been proven true.'

Morgan le Fay gets mentioned again two more times in *Erec and Enide*, once whilst Enide is making an offering at a Christian altar, and a second time in regards to an ointment that will heal Erec's badly wounded body,

> '... Then, on the altar, she offered green silk, such as had never been seen, and a large decorated chasuble [a type of cape favoured by priests] all embroidered in fine gold. It was a proven fact that Morgan le Fay had devoted all her skills to designing it at her home in the Perilous Vale. Made of gold and Almerian silk, it was not designed by le Fay to serve as a chasuble for singing the mass; not at all, for she wished to give it to her lover to make a splendid garment, since it was marvellously becoming.'

'...When they saw his wounds, joy turned to anger for the king [Arthur] *and all his people. The king then had an ointment brought out that had been made by Morgan, his sister. The ointment, which Morgan had given to Arthur, was so strong that within a week it would completely cure and heal the wound being treated, whether in the ligaments or the joints, provided the ointment was applied daily. The ointment, which was delivered to the king, brought Erec great relief.'*

And Morgan le Fay gets mentioned in another of Chrétien's stories (*The Knight with the Lion*),

'... "Take care now," the lady replied. "If he does not take flight, then certainly, with God's help, I believe we shall remove all the frenzy and insanity from his head. But we must set out immediately. I remember an ointment Morgan the Wise gave me, and she told me it would remove from the mind any grave illness." '

The mysterious lady, Morgen, first introduced in the *Vita Merlini* by Geoffrey of Monmouth (see pages 21-22); she who can fly anywhere at will, shape-shift, and is greatly gifted in the art of healing, has become 'le Fay' (the Fairy) in Chrétien's stories; he also states that she was Arthur's sister which is an important idea that I'll go into in more detail in Appendix VII.

Morgan le Fay remains enigmatic and illusive. Geoffrey of Monmouth described her as being beautiful and wrote full of admiration for her, her mystical sisterhood, and her otherworldly sanctuary, the 'Fortunate Isle'. Chrétien de Troyes never writes about her in any great detail but her presence is powerfully there, just behind the scenes, in his passing references already quoted above. She seems to be strikingly benevolent and kind, admired and respected, and yet in later Arthurian romances she will become portrayed as the dark nemesis of Arthur's kingdom, an evil sorceress conspiring to bring ruin to all; how did this come to be? We have already observed (on pages 44/45) how Gerald of Wales may have been cynical about the idea that Arthur rested in an otherworldly realm waiting to return again; and that to the Christian mind-set of the 12th and 13th centuries (and onwards) this could be considered demonic as only Jesus and the Virgin Mary had mysteriously, 'bodily', left this mortal world. If the passing of Arthur were true, that he went to some otherworldly place beyond the physical realm, then this was a spiritual affront to good Christianity; and Morgan le Fay was the figurehead of that otherworldly (non Christian) paradise.

Morgan le Fay may be a medieval variant of the Gaelic goddess of magic, shape-shifting, war and protection, the Morrigan. Her name can be translated as 'Great Queen' (*Mor-Rigan)* and she belongs to the same Celtic culture as the four treasures of sovereignty; the Sword of Nuada, the Spear of Lugh, the Cauldron of the Dagda, and the Stone of Destiny. The magical stories of Ireland (of the Gaelic Celts) are of course the enchanting stories of the all important 'furthest west' and Morrigan was the Great Queen of that Faerie realm in the direction of the setting sun.

More than the God-fearing anti-Semitic Catholic fervour of Robert de Boron and other later writers, the audience of Chrétien de Troyes (Marie of Champagne, Eleanor of Aquitaine, and others) were enthralled with the mystery and magic of the Faerie other-world. They sought stories of occultism, enchantment, and forbidden Mystery teachings. The following quote from Chrétien's story, *Erec and Enide* demonstrates this in full power; it comes from the end of the story when Erec and Enide become the king and queen of Brittany. The following quote may seem simple to modern readers but Geometry, Mathematics, Music, and Astronomy were seen as deeply esoteric sciences and the magnificent robe being described was made by four fairies; so it was a living thing of enchantment as it had not been made by human hands. This magical robe thus empowered Erec to govern Brittany (the furthest west) as an esoterically inspired and wise king,

'Four fairies had designed the robe with great skill and mastery. One embroidered the figure of Geometry there: examining and measuring the dimensions of the heavens and the earth, first the depth, then the height, then the width, then the length, so that nothing is missed, and afterwards examining the entire width and depth of the sea. Thereby measuring the entire world. This was the design of the first fairy.

The second fairy devoted her efforts to depicting, and worked hard to show clearly how Arithmetic wisely numbers days and hours of time, drops of water in the sea, and then all the grains of sand and the stars one by one. Arithmetic well knows how to tell the truth about this, and how many leaves there are in the forest; she has never been deceived in her numbers, and will never be mistaken in her calculation since she wished to put all her efforts into this. This was the design of Arithmetic.

The third design was that of Music where all pleasures find themselves in harmony: songs and counterpoints, and sounds of string, harp, violin, and viol. This was a beautiful and exquisite design, for in front of Music were depicted all the instruments and all the pleasures.

The fourth fairy, who toiled next, applied herself to a very fine design, for she depicted there the best of arts. She set her mind to the presentation of Astronomy, who accomplishes so many wonders under the inspiration of the stars, the moon, and the sun. From no other source does Astronomy take advice about anything she may have to do, for on whatever inquiry she makes, their counsel is good

*and proper, and free of lies and deceptions, about all that
was and all that will be.*

*This was the design figured and woven with gold thread on
the cloth of Erec's robe. The fur lining sewn inside came
from some strange beasts, which have heads completely
blonde and necks as black as mulberries, with scarlet
backs below, black stomachs, and dark-blue tails. Born in
India, such beasts are called berbiolettes and find their
only nourishment in fish, cinnamon, and fresh cloves.
What more can I tell you of the robe? It was costly, elegant,
and beautiful. In the tassels were four stones: two
chrysolites on one side and two amethysts on the other, all
set in gold.'*

(Chrétien de Troyes, *Erec and Enide*)

This fairy-made robe embodies the intellectual building-blocks of the scientific study of life, rather than the superstitious world-view of uneducated faith; the very rocks that a Renaissance Europe would be built upon. It would be a big mistake to think of fairies as tiny little Tinkerbells; one should rather imagine them as the immortal spirits of the Celtic otherworld assisting humanity.

Glastonbury's Joseph of Arimathea tradition is Christian and as such it is in defiance of any esoteric pagan lore; and the 'discovery' of King Arthur's grave specifically denies the existence of Morgan le Fay and the concept of a Celtic faerie other-world.

Percival

In Chrétien's *Le cont du Graal* Sir Percival is specifically described as 'a Welshman' and Chrétien also writes King Arthur swearing an oath, "... *by my lord Saint David, who is worshipped and prayed to in Wales.*" In *The High History of the Holy Graal* (see Appendix IV) it is claimed that the true history of the Graal was kept at Glastonbury Abbey; *'the whole history thereof, true from the beginning even to the end'*. The true origin of Glastonbury Abbey is that of Saint David and the Celtic Church of Wales; and Saint David's Sapphire Altar was the proto-Grail (from Jerusalem and upon which the lord had been sacrificed) that was celebrated by hundreds of visiting pilgrims more than fifty years before any of the fictional Grail Romances were even written down. The great pilgrimage to St David's was forgotten during the 12th century civil war known as The Anarchy; during which the countryside was literally burnt into a very real wasteland of Arthurian proportions. The castle of Castle Cary (an easy day's horse-ride from Glastonbury) belonged to the Perceval family during the devastation of the land under The Anarchy. From the site of Castle Cary's castle the one thing that dominates the horizon fourteen miles away is Glastonbury Tor. The Perceval family would have looked out upon the Tor every day. In 1184 Glastonbury Abbey burnt down and in 1191 the monks claimed to discover King Arthur's grave; that same year Richard the Lionheart gave Excalibur to the king of Sicily. In Sicily with King Richard was Philip the Count of Flanders; the very person that gave the story of the Graal to Chrétien de Troyes to transcribe into poetic romance. A decade or so later Robert de Boron added the fictional back-story of Joseph of Arimathea to the growing mass of Grail stories and then an unknown person added Joseph of Arimathea into Glastonbury's 'tradition'. The rest, as they say, is history.

Chretien de Troyes came from Burgundy; Robert de Boron came from Burgundy; and the most likely true location for the mythical Avalon are the hills and forests of the Avallonnais around the modern town of Avallon which still exists in Burgundy today.

Sir Percival

From the Well Maidens of the Summerlands project

www.wellmaidens.co.uk

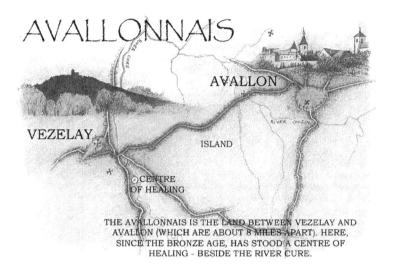

AVALLONNAIS

AVALLON

VEZELAY

ISLAND

CENTRE
OF HEALING

THE AVALLONNAIS IS THE LAND BETWEEN VEZELAY AND
AVALLON (WHICH ARE ABOUT 8 MILES APART). HERE,
SINCE THE BRONZE AGE, HAS STOOD A CENTRE OF
HEALING - BESIDE THE RIVER CURE.

Remains of the ancient sanctuary of healing
beside the River Cure
below Vézelay
in the Avallonnais

CHAPTER FOUR
~ *THE MYSTERIES OF AVALLON* ~

'The mythic island where Arthur goes is a paradisal 'Place of Apples' or 'Apple Orchard', or so the name is generally taken to mean – certainly by Geoffrey. In Welsh it is Ynys Avallach. Geoffrey's Latin equivalent is 'Insula Avallonis'. But this is not really equivalent since it doesn't correspond to the Welsh. It has been influenced by the spelling of a real place called Avallon. Avallon is a Gaulish name with the same meaning, and the real Avallon is in Burgundy.'

(Geoffrey Ashe, *The Discovery of King Arthur*)

Avallon is a very old town, most probably pre-Roman, and it is situated in the Yonne department of modern day Burgundy in France. Romano-Gallic coins have been found there with the word *ABALLO* written upon them (*B* and *V* were inter-changeable in the Celtic languages). The town of Avallon gives its name to a wide area of forest between itself and the sacred hill of Vézelay; and the area between the two places is called the Avallonnais.

The old Clock Tower in the heart of the Old Town area of Avallon.
The Clock Tower also served as a watchtower in days gone by.

Flowing through the Avallonnais, below Vézelay, is the River Cure. Cure is a French word and it means exactly what you would expect it to mean; a healing. By this river of healing, and very close to Vézelay, are the remains of a very ancient healing sanctuary; which archaeologists have given the most unimaginative name of Les Fontaines Salées (the salt-water springs).

One of the salt-water springs of Les Fontaines Salées,
in the Avallonnais by the River Cure;
Still bubbling with warm healing waters.

Roman remains at Les Fontaines Salées;
but use of the site dates back to the Bronze Age.

In pre-Roman times the Avallonnais belonged to the territory of a Celtic tribe called the Aedui. The image below is an archaeological plan of the healing sanctuary. On the lower right-hand side can be seen the circular temple, with a salt-water spring in its centre, of the Celtic people. Everything else is Roman and this map clearly shows how the Romans just built on top of the older Celtic sanctuary.

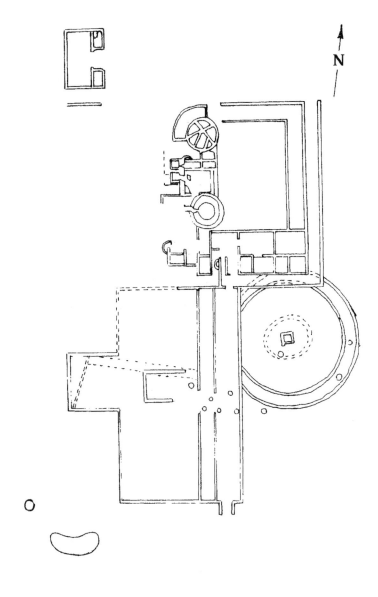

The roman remains at Les Fontaines Salées mark it out as a high-status Gallo-Roman 'Thermal establishment'; we might call it a Health Spa. There were many rooms for all of the various types of bathing that the Romans liked to experience; even a 'women only' area for beauty treatments.

Les Fontaines Salées were only discovered in the last century; because they had been deliberately concealed in medieval times.

It was in 1934 that René Louis, a French professor from Nanterre University in Paris, decided to excavate the site. He initially thought that the uneven ground may have concealed castle ruins but it turned out to be Roman remains. When I first started investigating online I found a tourist website called **burgundytoday.com** upon which the sanctuary was described as,

'A centre of healing in Roman times and a druidic college in pre-Roman times'.

I have not found any evidence of it being a druidic college but it was certainly a sacred site to the Celts so their spiritual leaders would have been there of course; whether it was a place where young people trained to be druids how could that be known? But it's a nice idea. It wasn't until 2013 that I was able to visit the salt-water springs for myself and discover just how very old the site actually was. The old salt-water springs near the circular Celtic area were deliberately lined with fire-hollowed oak trunks which have been carbon-dated to four and a half thousand years ago, circa 2500 BC; making them truly ancient even to the Aedui and their druids.

The site of Les Fontaines Salées was left to ruin after the collapse of the Roman empire. The springs remained as a useful source of in-land salt for local people (this being central France and a long way from any coastline); until the 14th century when the monks of Vézelay Abbey covered over the springs to prevent people from extracting the salt which was then subject to a tax called *la Gabelle*. Once covered over the sanctuary remained hidden until René Louis began excavating in the 1930s. Then World War Two happened. It is only in the last 70 years or so that the significance of this important site has begun to be appreciated.

Glastonbury author and respected Arthurian scholar, Geoffrey Ashe, promoted Avallon in Burgundy as the real Avalon as early as 1985; in his book *The Discovery of King Arthur* (which seems to have fallen, for the most part, upon deaf ears in Glastonbury). His *Discovery of King Arthur* was largely dismissed by most Arthurian scholars as his Arthur, an early British king called Riothamus, could not have been the Arthur at the all important Battle of Badon. Mr Ashe suggests that Riothamus was 'an' Arthur and that he was 'the' Arthur that ended his days in Avallon, Burgundy. Geoffrey Ashe speculates that it was the memory of Riothamus that inspired Geoffrey of Monmouth's 12th century fictional story about King Arthur being taken to the '*insula Afallonis*' to be healed of his wounds.

Geoffrey Ashe's Riothamus theory was taken up by another writer, Marilyn Floyde, and Mr Ashe wrote a foreword for her book, *King Arthur's French Odyssey: Avallon in Burgundy*.

The website, burgundytoday.com, promotes the 'Arthur-Riothamus' theories of Geoffrey Ashe and Marilyn Floyde. For myself, I do not think that Riothamus was **the** Arthur but I do think that it is most likely that the memory of the healing sanctuary, by the River Cure in the Avallonnais, became a magical and otherworldly realm of healing in the cultural folk-memory of the Norman French story-tellers.

For certain, the concept of warm salt-water springs being a gift of nature for healing the body, was an idea that Geoffrey of Monmouth contemplated; In his *Vita Merlini* he has Taliesin describe the exact phenomenon to Merlin (albeit he is describing the healing waters of the city of Bath),

> *'Besides all these it has fountains healthful because of their hot waters which nourish the sick and provide pleasing baths, which quickly send people away cured with their sickness driven out...*
> *... these are of value to many sick because of the healing of their water, but most of all to women, as often the water has demonstrated.'*
> (Geoffrey of Monmouth, *Vita Merlini*, circa 1150)

Les Fontaines Salées, just like the famous Roman baths of Bath, were a significant Roman establishment in the heart of France; but sadly mostly destroyed.

VÉZELAY

The hill-top town of Vézelay

The Abbaye Sainte-Marie-Madeleine de Vézelay

'If the vitality of Normandy flows through the channels of the seas, the life of Burgundy runs through the ways of the land. Michelet has said, 'France has no element more binding than Burgundy, more capable of reconciling North and South.' It lies at the centre of the river-system of France, and so has been from time immemorial a centre of trade. The fairs of Châlon, Auton, Dijon, Auxonne, Beaune, Châtillon, and Tonnerre carried on a commercial tradition dating from Carolingian and even Roman times. But besides being the home of commerce, it was the home of religion; its abbeys – Cluny, Citeaux, Clairvaux, Vézelay, Flavigny, Tournus, St Pierre de Bèze, Pothières, Saint Benigne de Dijon, and the rest – were not only important in themselves but did much to bring religion into feudal life.'
(Joan Evans, *Life in Medieval France*)

The preceding quote highlights the importance of Burgundy (and thus the Avallonnais) even during Roman times. The town of Avallon (or *ABALLO* as it was then known) was situated upon the Via Agrippa; one of the important Roman roads that ran through Gaul.

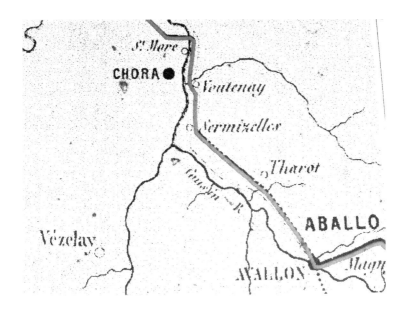

Part of the Via Agrippa; the Roman road that runs through Burgundy; connecting *ABALLO* to *CHORA*.

On the hill of Vézelay, during the 17th century, a Roman temple of Bacchus was found (the hill had been used by the Romans to grow grapevines). Bacchus was the god of wine; but more than this, as the Roman equivalent of Dionysus, Bacchus was a god of the ancient Mystery traditions.

'At the heart of the Mysteries were myths concerning a dying and resurrecting godman, who was known by many different names. In Egypt he was Osiris, in Greece Dionysus, in Asia Minor Attis, in Syria Adonis, in Italy Bacchus, in Persia Mithras.'
(Timothy Freke & Peter Gandy, *The Jesus Mysteries*)

Bacchus was very popular in Roman settlements and his shrines were often close to places where Mithras was worshipped. The Mystery rites of Mithras were very popular with the Roman legionaries and a pottery head of Mithras was found at *CHORA* just up along the Via Agrippa from Avallon (see map on the previous page).

'It is interesting to note that Bacchus is frequently found in connection with other deities, in reliefs or statues at their temples. Thus we see three marble statues of Bacchus found at the London Mithraeum, images of him at the baths at Aquae Sulis and a lead plaque at the temple of Nodens at Lydney (Gloucestershire).'
(David Rankine & Sorita D'Este, *The Isles of the Many Gods*)

Most Mystery rituals and secret rites used wine, of course (even Jesus turned water into wine), so Bacchus was ever-present wherever sacred wine was needed. The importance of Mithras and other Mystery traditions is their extensive use of very complicated star-lore for teaching esoteric wisdom concepts; and the Avallonnais is full of zodiacal intrigues which we'll come to shortly.

Vézelay Abbey was founded in the 9th century and like Glastonbury Abbey it belonged to the Benedictine order. It became very famous from about 1035 AD onwards when it began to claim that it was the final resting place for the body of Mary Magdalene. The history of the Magdalene cult throughout the medieval era is very complicated and it is as dubious as the Joseph of Arimathea tradition of England. Both 'traditions' were of course created to give each abbey (and country) a direct apostolic succession from Jesus himself. Joseph gathered the blood of Jesus during (or just after) the crucifixion and Mary Magdalene was the very first person that Jesus is said to have appeared to after his resurrection. England and France were thus attempting to establish stronger apostolic succession claims than that of the Vatican itself (which was established by Saint Peter).

'Therefore it seems that the crusade against the Cathars, which continued for another thirty-five years, was to some extent a cover for the suppression of the Church of Mary Magdalene. Both heresies were rooted out with unprecedented ferocity.

It was within a few years of the end of the Cathar Crusade that the most famous version of the legends of the Magdalene's life in France appeared, Jacobus de Voragine's 'The Golden Legend', which we have noted earlier. Significantly, Jacobus was a Dominican – and the Dominicans were the Inquisition. Coming so soon after the crusade in southern France, it seems that the purpose of his account was to subvert the popular French traditions about Mary Magdalene by producing a version that was more in keeping with the Church's image of her. They realised that although the crusade had eradicated her cult as a coherent movement or organisation, her story would continue to circulate in the heretical subculture, so it had to be 'hijacked'. The process of taking control of the Magdalene cult was completed by establishing an 'official' cult and pilgrimage centre at Saint-Maximin-la-Sainte-Baume, the legendary scene of her death.

Until 1279 – again, in the wake of the Cathar Crusade – the Church's endorsement had been given to the relics of Mary Magdalene at Vézelay in Burgundy. Even these had a link with the south, as they had been taken from there to Vézelay by the Count of Roussillon in the 9th century. (It was from Vézelay that Bernard of Clairvaux had called for the Second Crusade.) But in 1279 a skeleton in an alabaster sarcophagus – allegedly of Mary Magdalene – was discovered beneath the crypt of the church in Saint-Maximin. A document found in the sarcophagus stated that her body had been reburied some 460 years before to protect it from invading 'Saracens'. (It is now known that *this document is a fake – in part because there were no Saracen invasions in the 8th century – but it was believed at the time. Of course, if the document was faked, then undoubtedly so was the body). The pope officially favoured these relics over those at Vézelay, and in 1295 authorized the building of the basilica that would serve as a centre for pilgrims. The skull was removed and is still displayed in the basilica today – which grins out of its ornate reliquary like a comment on human vanity and the ephemeral nature of mortality – and is paraded around the town annually to celebrate Mary Magdalene's feast day, encased in a handsome gold mask topped by a bandeau from which cascade shiny and ludicrously blonde locks.*

The pope also placed the basilica under his direct control – not, as was customary, under that of the local archbishop – and replaced the Benedictine monks that were installed there with Dominicans. Effectively, the Magdalene cult and pilgrimage centre was placed under the control of the Inquisition. It is for this reason that St Mary Magdalene was made patron saint of the Dominicans (in 1297), and declared to be the 'daughter, sister and mother' to the Order.'

(Lynn Picknett, *Mary Magdalene: Christianity's Hidden Goddess*)

As I have already stated, the history of the cult of Mary Magdalene in France is very complicated. For those readers that are interested in exploring the topic further I highly recommend the deeply fascinating book, *Mary Magdalene: Christianity's Hidden Goddess* by Lynn Picknett. Generally it would appear that, as the many pagan Mystery traditions of the Roman Empire clearly influenced early Christianity, behind the Magdalene cult are to be found the Mystery traditions of the Egyptian goddess Isis. As for Mary Magdalene's relics being kept at Vézelay (as is still claimed) or at Saint-Maximin (or neither) the reader must decide for themselves. The goddess Isis is Queen of Heaven and both the Virgin Mary and Mary Magdalene are often depicted surrounded by stars - making now a good time to look at the intriguing star-lore to be found in the Avallonnais.

STAR-LORE

The ornate zodiacal entrance to the
Abbaye Sainte-Marie-Madeleine de Vézelay
(see photograph on page 57 to see it in its full context).

Close up detail, from left to right:
Cancer the Crab, the Triple Melusine, and Leo the Lion.

The zodiacal arch of Vézelay is very ornate, and its details are deteriorating, but the full zodiac is there interspaced between small scenes of seasonal activities like sewing, reaping, and harvesting etc. The zodiac is a common enough decoration that is found in many churches and abbeys. That which is uniquely interesting at Vézelay is the placement of Cancer and Leo to the left and the right of the head of Jesus. There are many ways of displaying the twelve signs of the zodiac, the most common is from Aries (Spring Equinox) through to Pisces (the end of the zodiacal year), but the zodiac of Vézelay begins with Aquarius (at the bottom left) and concludes with Capricorn (at the bottom right). The zodiacal layout of Vézelay is a Mystery tradition system inherited from the Roman Empire. The exact same layout can be seen around a figure of Mithras found at Hadrian's Wall in Britain.

The Mithraic 'Rock-Birth' from Hadrian's Wall.

Just like the zodiac of Vézelay, this Mithraic zodiac begins with Aquarius (at the bottom left) and concludes with Capricorn (at the bottom right). Cancer the Crab and Leo the Lion are situated just above Mithras' head; just as they do above Jesus at Vézelay (Cancer has been defaced).

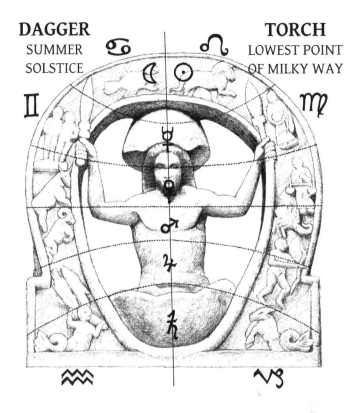

Here is a glimpse into Mithraic complexity. Cancer the Crab is the only zodiac sign governed by the moon and Leo is the only sign governed by the sun; so symbolically the moon and the sun are in position to shine a direct influence upon Mithras' mind. The remaining zodiac signs share a planetary influence that correspond (chakra-like) with the various levels of his body. Gemini & Virgo are ruled by Mercury; Taurus & Libra are by Venus; Aries & Scorpio correspond with Mars; Pisces & Sagittarius, Jupiter; and Aquarius & Capricorn with Saturn. At the top, Mercury and Venus are the closest planets to the sun, whilst Mars, Jupiter, and Saturn are furthest away (or deeper into the darker depths of Space rather than closer towards the light). Saturn corresponds with the depths of winter, the

Roman festival of Saturnalia, from whence (just like Jesus) Mithras is born. His sword points at the summer solstice.

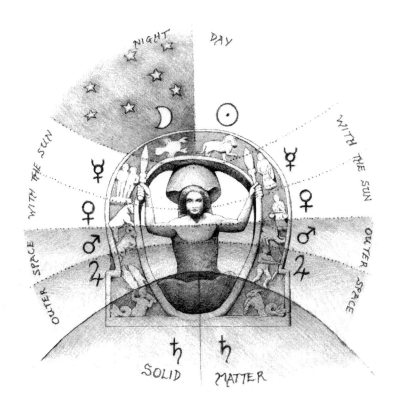

Being born at midwinter is not the only similarity that this image of Mithras shares with Jesus. Jesus is often described as the 'Alpha and the Omega' (the beginning and the end of the Greek alphabet). In the image above, look carefully, Mithras sits within a giant Omega (in this case it represents the all encompassing circle of Time and totality). The moon and sun equate with day and night which suggests the dual nature of one's mind (whether the modern left-brain right-brain knowledge or the concept of one's conscious and subconscious self). The exact centre-point, the space between Cancer and Leo, corresponds with the first degree of Leo (the 22nd of July; or in the Christian calendar of saints, the feast day of Mary Magdalene - which is something very curious to ponder in regards to the zodiacal arch of Vézelay). Mithras holds the tip of his sword between Gemini and Cancer (the position of summer solstice) and we have already observed that as Jesus was given the winter solstice, John the Baptist was given the summer solstice, and one of his hallows is the sword that decapitated him (Mithras also gives us a sword at summer solstice). All these pre-Christian elements are found in just one, rather rustic, carving that the Romans left behind on Hadrian's Wall; across the empire there were thousands.

The nave of Vézelay is lit up by the midday sun,
every summer solstice, for the feast of John the Baptist.

The zodiacal lore of the Mithras image becomes even more complicated but it will shed light upon the Triple

Melusine between Cancer and Leo at Vézelay. Whilst Mithras points to summer solstice (between Gemini and Cancer) he also points to the cusp between Leo and Virgo with his torch; why? Remember, the most important lesson in the story of Sir Percival is, whenever anything unusual is shown to you always ask 'Why?'. A torch is needed when one descends into the dark depths of the lowest part of the Milky Way (we have already encountered 'The Deep' as the 'Milky Way Spirit-path' on page 59).

VIRGO ~ MELUSINE
At the lowest part of the Milky Way

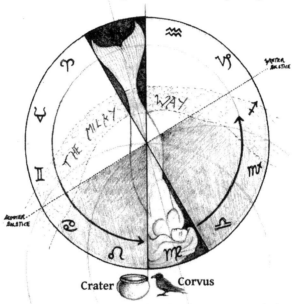

The Milky Way can be seen as the path of souls.
After death (Scorpio) souls ascend into the spirit world,
the route, the arrow-shot from Sagittarius to Gemini, then souls
descend back into the world of matter. At Crater, the
Cauldron of Renewal, Melusine oversees the cycle repeat again.

Virgo is the dark goddess of the Mysteries. In the classical world she corresponded with the Mystery goddesses of initiation, Demeter and Ceres (and in the Welsh, post Romano-British bardic tradition, Ceres became Ceridwen); she may even be seen as the Great Queen (the

'Mor-Rigan') of the Celtic other-world; with the constellation of Corvus the Crow being Morrigan's totem, the Raven.

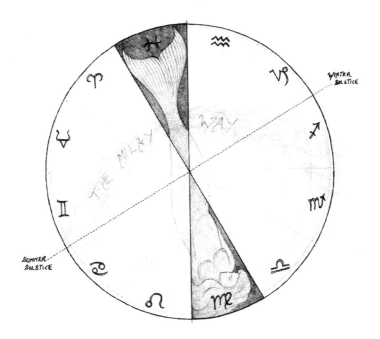

Virgo, the lowest point of the Milky way, and its opposite sign Pisces the highest part of the Milky Way, create the celestial mermaid (half maiden half fish). This is the heavenly origin of the otherworldly mermaid, mystery figure, Melusine; of whom Richard the Lionheart and the the Angevin bloodline believed they were descended.

'But remarkable though they were, his English forefathers seem to have meant little to Richard himself – and this despite the fact that the old Germanic god of war was among their number. When he jokingly referred to the story that he was descended from the Devil he meant no disrespect to his ancestor Woden. He was referring to an Angevin legend, the story of Mélusine. She was a lady of unearthly beauty who married a Count of Anjou and bore him four children. Everything about her marriage seemed to be perfect, apart from one disquieting fact: she hated going into churches and she absolutely refused to be

present at the consecration of the Host. Jealous voices reminded the Count of this again and again; eventually he decided to put her to the test. He summoned her to attend church and then, at the moment of consecration, just as she was about to leave, four armed men stopped her. But as they seized her by the mantle, she shook it from her shoulders, folded two of her children in her arms and floated away through a window, never more to be seen by her husband and the two children she left behind.'
(John Gillingham, *Richard The Lionheart*)

The above version of the Melusine story plays upon her apparent aversion to Christianity but it is not the only variation of her story; there is a much more detailed version in *Curious Myths of the Middle Ages*, compiled by the Rev. Sabine Baring-Gould. In the *Curious Myths* there is no mention of aversion to Christianity but rather a pact with the faerie world that was broken. Melusine was one of three beautiful water spirits that the Count of Anjou encountered in a forest.

'Presently the boughs of the trees became less interlaced and the trunks fewer, and, next moment, his horse crashed through the shrubs and brought him out on a pleasant glade, white with rime and illumined by the new moon. In the midst bubbled up a limpid fountain and flowed away over a pebbly floor with a soothing murmur. Near the fountain-head sat three maidens in glimmering white dresses, with long waving golden hair and faces of inexpressible beauty.
Raymond was riveted to the spot with astonishment. He believed that he saw a vision of angels and would have prostrated himself at their feet had not one of them advanced and stayed him.'
(Sabine Baring-Gould, *Curious Myths of the Middle Ages*)

The young Count and the water-spirit, Melusine, fell in love and she agreed to marry him but only on the condition that every Saturday she must have her own privacy. They lived happily ever after and had many children until one sad day when curiosity got the better of Count Raymond and he spied upon Melusine,

'One Saturday the old father inquired at dinner after his daughter-in-law. Raymond replied that she was not visible on Saturdays. Thereupon one of his brothers, drawing him aside, whispered that strange gossiping tales were about relative to this Sabbath seclusion, and that it behoved him to inquire into it and set the minds of the people at rest.
Full of wrath and anxiety, the Count rushed off to the private apartments of the countess, but found them empty. One door alone was locked, and that opened into a bath. He looked through the key-hole and to his dismay beheld her in the water, her lower extremities changed into the tail of a monstrous fish or serpent.'
(Sabine Baring-Gould, *Curious Myths of the Middle Ages*)

It is clear from the description of the three well maidens in *Curious Myths of the Middle Ages* that Melusine was a nature spirit; more specifically a Water Nymph (which were often depicted in threes). Compare the three Water Nymphs below (from Hadrian's Wall) with the Triple Melusine on the zodiacal arch of Vézelay (on the next page).

The Triple Melusine of Vézelay.

However one interprets the above image it is a very odd set of symbols to place directly above the head of Jesus (as it is a Vézelay); between Cancer and Leo (the moon and the sun) and corresponding with the specific time of year that is the feast of Mary Magdalene. More simply, are they Water Nymphs that acknowledge the sacred salt-water springs in the healing sanctuary by the River Cure just below Vézelay?

There is still much to explore. The world is transitioning from the Age of Pisces into the Age of Aquarius; Melusine is the hidden goddess of the Age of Pisces (the fish are her tail). She lies in the deep waters of space, this celestial lady of the lake. As already mentioned, she may be the origin of the Great Queen, (Mor-Rigan) and even the word 'Fay' is Norman French in origin (and derived from the pagan Roman culture of Celtic Gaul).

'Some discussion as to the origin of the term "fairy" is an essential preliminary to the study of fairy lore in general...
... The great majority of those writers who have faithfully examined the origin of the word "fairy" are of the opinion that it was distantly derived from the Latin noun 'fatum', or "fate", that is the word which describes those goddesses, the 'Fatæ'...
... in later Roman Gaul it also took the form 'fata'. There, in accordance with a law of Celtic phonetics, the "t" was slurred, or elided, which gave it the sound of "fa'a", and in

the plural "fa'ae". This, later, in early French, came to be pronounced as 'fa'èe', and still later as 'fèe', from which, again, came the English "Fay", almost certainly the product of Norman-French influence.'
(Lewis Spence, *The Fairy Tradition in Britain*)

For now, within the near presence of Morgan 'le Fay', and the knowledge that she was always something other than mere human, let's go back to the town of Avallon for it too has some curious zodiacal intrigues.

The ornate entrance to the church of Sainte-Lazare, in the Old Town area of Avallon.

In 2013 I had the good fortune of being able to visit Avallon and Vézelay for myself thanks to my friends Mandy and Kevin who took me on holiday with them; we spent eleven memorable days driving all over France. We were only in the town of Avallon for just one a day; just long enough to observe that the entrance to the church of Sainte-Lazare (above) was decorated with the signs of the zodiac. Also, curiously, whilst walking around Avallon's external fortified walls (which have many towers and turrets) we found the twelve signs of the zodiac embedded into one of the old battlements.

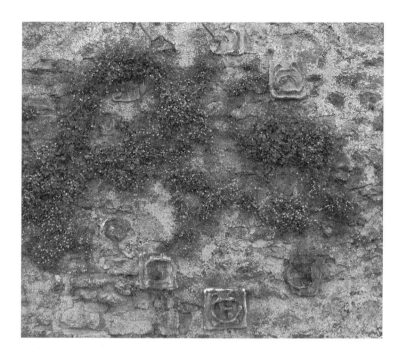

We were not there long enough to find out how old this wall zodiac was but the carvings were quite eroded. Here is a close-up of the Scorpio figure (at the ten o'clock position in the picture above). I hope to return to Avallon one day if the Fates allow.

It was a potent seed in my mind, that the scorpion was the best preserved of the Avallon wall zodiac signs. It stayed in my mind along with a random piece of knowledge that I had picked up along the way – that the name of the hill of Vézelay was Scorpion Hill. (Why Sir Percival?) If it was not for the scorpion in the wall I may never have given the place-name of Scorpion Hill so much contemplation.

After visiting the Avallonnais my friends and I then drove to Bourges. On the way there a major stretch of the journey seemed to be along very straight Roman roads. As I sat in the back of the car, thinking about Scorpion Hill, it dawned on me that there may be a straight line (Roman road) connection from Vézelay to Bourges; and indeed there was although it took me a while to piece it all together and the result made complete sense of the place-name Scorpion Hill.

THE SCORPION LINE

My friend, the author Andrew Collins, had written about Bourges in his book *Twenty-first Century Grail*.

"Not only does it stand at the geographical centre of France, but Bourges is also equidistant from three other French cathedrals, which form a perfect triangle around it. They are Gisors to the north, Jarnac to the southwest and Montrevel to the east, all of them with supposed links to the Knights Templar."

Bourges certainly was a very important place. It was the capital city of Aquitaine (the home turf of Richard I's mother, Eleanor of Aquitaine). In Roman times it was known as *AVARICUM* and it was indeed connected to Vézelay by Roman roads. More than this, Bourges is the sacred omphalos or heart-centre of France. Bourges has many meaningful connections of interest for Earth Mysteries investigators (including its situation upon the great alignments known as the Apollo Line and the Rose Line); too many intrigues to be covered in this book.

Map from Andrew Collins' book *Twenty-first Century Grail*; shows Bourges at the centre of France. The Apollo Line from St Michael's Mount in Cornwall, and the Rose Line running through Paris, cross each other at Bourges.

In Andrew's book he wrote that Bourges was the,

'... sacred centre of the country, seen by its indigenous Celtic peoples as the dead centre not just of France, but of the whole world. In this role, Bourges would have been venerated as a pivot or cosmic axis, symbolized by the royal seat of the 'king of the world', around which revolved the starry firmament, its rhythmic movement regulating the passage of time.'
(Andrew Collins, *Twenty-first Century Grail*)

Andrew's words, *'around which revolved the starry*

firmament' got me pondering; could Scorpion Hill (Vézelay) correspond with the sign of Scorpio if Bourges were the centre-point of a vast zodiac? Yes, and it made the Paris Meridian (the Rose Line), due north, correspond with the first degree of Capricorn (the all important winter solstice).

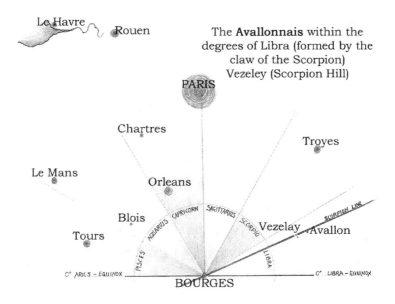

If you place the wheel of the zodiac with its centre-point upon Bourges and align the two equinox points (zero degrees Aries and zero degrees Libra) due east and west, then Vézelay, the Scorpion Hill, falls within the angle of Libra, close to the cusp of Scorpio. At first this may appear to be a failed 'hit' but we know (from the writings of Ptolemy) that once, the entire constellation of Scorpio was so huge that it took up the space of two sections of the zodiac so the scales of Libra were created from the scorpion's claws.

As illustrated on page 104, Scorpio is important as the beginning of the journey along the Milky Way spirit-path. This heavenly passage is the real meaning of the pilgrimage to Compostela (which means 'Field of Stars', the Milky Way) thus, starting the great pilgrimage from the Scorpion Hill is an obvious representation of 'as above so below'.

The most astounding thing about the Scorpion Line from the Avallonnais is that if you project the line from Vézelay through Bourges and keep going then it will end at Finisterre ('the end of the earth') at the end of the Camino de Santiago de Compostela. See the map on page 19 to appreciate this truly astounding terrestrial alignment that divides France into a huge terrestrial zodiac.

See the map on page 19

* * *

The Avallonnais: a town called Avallon, a healing sanctuary that dates back to the Bronze Age, a river called the Cure, Water Nymphs and a temple of Bacchus Dionysus, zodiacal mysteries and terrestrial alignments; in Burgundy, the source of the Grail romances, and the home of Chrétien de Troyes and Robert de Boron.

What is Glastonbury to make of all of this? Glastonbury belonged to the Angevin Empire (whilst it lasted) and the Angevin royal family promoted the Arthurian and Grail romances as it pleased them.

And what of the spirits of the land and the Celtic ancestral spirits of the Avallonnais, the Aedui and their druids?

The forests still breathe and grow,
The rivers still glisten and flow,
The stars still shine in the sky,
And Morgan le Fay
is just a whisper away.

* * *

The Lady Kundry,
Maiden of the Grail.

From the Well Maidens of the Summerlands project

www.wellmaidens.co.uk

~ APPENDICES ~

The Lady Elaine.

From the Well Maidens of the Summerlands project

www.wellmaidens.co.uk

APPENDIX I
GLASTONBURY'S ARTHURIAN TIME-LINE

1090 ~ Rhygyfarch's *Life of David* stated that Saint David built the first church in Glastonbury; this would have been during the 500s and contemporary with the historical Arthur.

1123 ~ Pope Callixtus II declared St. David's to be a sacred pilgrimage destination; three visits to St. David's were equal to one visit to Jerusalem.

1124 ~ Henry of Blois, abbot of Glastonbury, just happened to find the 'Sapphire Altar' which Saint David had received in Jerusalem; the sacred relic, proto-Grail, that Jesus had been sacrificed upon.

1135 ~ William of Malmesbury's *Antiquities of Glastonbury* explained the discovery of the Sapphire Altar; ensuring that Glastonbury (the first church that Saint David established) would be a primary centre of worship for pilgrims on their way to St. David's.

1136 ~ Geoffrey of Monmouth's (fictional) *History of the Kings of Britain* was the first detailed Life of King Arthur and the first ever mention of the Isle of Avalon, Merlin, Queen Guinevere, and Excalibur. It described Arthur as 'our renowned king'.

1155 ~ Caradoc of Llancarfon's *Life of Gildas* is the very first account of King Arthur visiting Glastonbury. Arthur is said to have brought an army to Glastonbury to rescue Guinevere; she was a captive of King Melvas of the Summer Country (and he held her prisoner in Glastonbury). St Gildas and the abbot of Glastonbury intervened to stop bloodshed between the two kings. It is a fictional story written to secure Glastonbury Abbey certain land rights.

1191 ~ The year claimed by the abbot of Glastonbury (Richard I's nephew) for the discovery of King Arthur's grave. This same year Richard gave a sword he claimed was Excalibur to the king of Sicily. With Richard in Sicily was Philip the Count of Flanders; who had commissioned Chrétien de Troyes to write the first story of the Graal.

1193 ~ The first eye-witness account of King Arthur's grave being discovered in Glastonbury is written by Gerald of Wales. Gerald states that the lead cross read 'our renowned king' which is a phrase taken directly from the writing of Geoffrey of Monmouth (see 1136 above).

1200s (early) ~ Robert de Boron's *Joseph D'Arimathe* declares the Grail to be the Cup of the Last Supper (Later Grail writers continue this tradition and Joseph of Arimathea becomes a popular figure).

1211-1223 ~ The *Chronicle of Hélinand* explains the meaning of the French word 'Graal'; it is a type of serving dish and it implies stages of initiation via Mystery rites.

1220 (circa) ~ *The High History of the Holy Grail* specifically states that the true history of the story of the Grail was kept at Glastonbury Abbey; *'at the head of the Moors Adventurous, there where King Arthur and Queen Guinevere lie.'*

1240 (circa) ~ An unknown writer adds the spurious *Charter of the Blessed Patrick* material to *The Antiquities of Glastonbury*; in simple terms, Glastonbury's Joseph of Arimathea 'tradition' was invented.

1278 – King Edward I and his queen visit Glastonbury and place the claimed bones of Arthur and Guinevere into a black marble tomb (placed near the high altar of Glastonbury abbey).

* * *

The Lady Dindraine.

From the Well Maidens of the Summerlands project

www.wellmaidens.co.uk

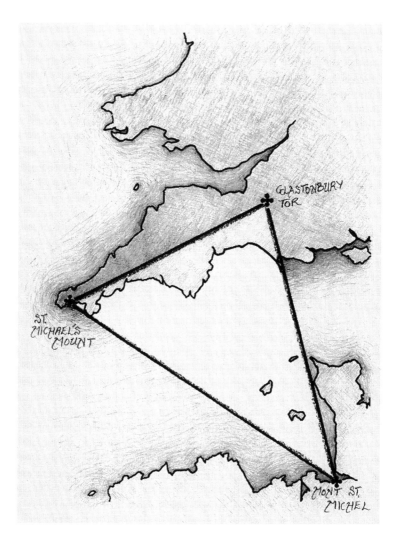

The medieval Benedictine intrigue of the
Triangle of Michael.

APPENDIX II
BENEDICTINE INTRIGUES

We have already observed (on pages 112 and 113) vast terrestrial alignments running across France; the Apollo Line and the Rose Line crossing each other at Bourges (the heart-centre of France) and the Scorpion Line that runs from the Avallonnais, through Bourges, to Finisterre at the end of the Camino de Santiago de Compostela in Spain. These fascinating Earth Mysteries are just the tip of the proverbial iceberg. In England we have the Benedictine enigma of the Triangle of Michael (see opposite) and other more curious terrestrial phenomena. There is only space in this short appendix to take a quick glimpse; for further information about the Triangle of Michael and other landscape patterns around Glastonbury I refer the reader to my book *The Terrestrial Alignments of Katharine Maltwood and Dion Fortune.*

In the 1930s, the occult author Dion Fortune, in her novel *The Goat Foot God*, described the Triangle of Michael shown on the opposite page. Each corner of the triangle is a powerful site that was dedicated to the archangel Michael by the Benedictine order – Glastonbury Tor, Mont-St-Michel in Normandy, and Saint Michael's Mount in Cornwall. The three sides of this enigmatic triangle project three great terrestrial alignments:

The St Michael Line
St Michael's Mount through Glastonbury Tor
passes through many sacred sites including Avebury.
The Apollo Line
St Michael's Mount through Mont-St-Michel
passes through many sacred sites including Bourges.
The Ogmios Line
Mont-St-Michel through Glastonbury Tor
passes through many sacred sites including Callanish.

The evidence does seem to imply that the Benedictine order had an esoteric interest in terrestrial alignments and ancient places of power. Benedictine monasteries were known for their great libraries; which contained not just books of the faith but also salvaged knowledge from the classical pagan past. Many early churches were built upon the sites of older pagan worship and so many of these great alignments must be pre-Roman in origin and thousands of years old. The study of these terrestrial alignments and other patterns across the land is now know as Earth Mysteries. Some of these alignments point towards specific sunrises (like the St. Michael Line which points to the sunrise of Beltaine) and others are more obscure and may align with the moon or specific constellations; or they may simply have been fire-beacon communication routes. Both Vézelay and Glastonbury were very important Benedictine power-houses and they were both spiritually active in pre-Christian Roman times; Vézelay had a temple of Bacchus and the ancient healing sanctuary, and Glastonbury Tor has evidence of a Romano-British pagan temple.

Understanding the cycle of the year is a major key to understanding many of these Mysteries; see image at the top of the next page. The two pillars represent the winter solstice and the summer solstice; the shortest day of the year and the longest day of the year. The mid-point between the two pillars is the equinox line which defines the days of equal lengths of light and darkness; the spring equinox and the autumn equinox. This natural cycle of Time divides the year into two halves (the dark half and the light half in the illustration opposite). This binary division of the year was used by some ancient Mystery Traditions to teach certain esoteric concepts. The imaginal grid of the zodiac divides the circle of the year into twelve equal sections; each section is thirty degrees wide (12 x 30 = 360 degrees). The imaginal zodiacal grid is fixed to the four exact stations of the sun; the two solstices and the two equinoxes (and it is called the Sun Cross; see page 59).

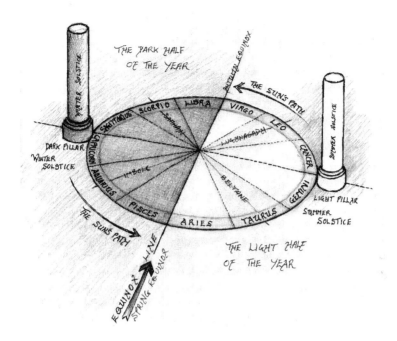

THE SUN CROSS

Winter Solstice ~ Sun at zero degrees Capricorn.
Spring Equinox ~ Sun at zero degrees Aries.
Summer Solstice ~ Sun at zero degrees Cancer.
Autumn Equinox ~ Sun at zero degrees Libra.

The mid-points between the four arms of the Sun Cross were observed by the Celtic people and can thus be assumed to have been a part of the star-lore of the ancient druids. The four 'cross-quarter' festivals are,

Imbolc ~ Sun at 15 degrees of Aquarius.
Beltaine ~ Sun at 15 degrees of Taurus.
Lughnasadh ~ Sun at 15 degrees of Leo.
Samhain ~ Sun at 15 degrees of Scorpio.

The four Celtic cross-quarter festivals also define the Royal Star Cross of the Mystery Traditions (see page 60).

The winter solstice and the summer solstice are known as the 'two pillars of the temple' and are seen as holding the heavenly kingdom aloft; and these two pillars were absorbed into Christianity in a most fascinating way. Nowhere in the Bible does it say that Jesus was born on the 25th December; his birth date is not given at all. Who decided upon the 25th December and why?

'Examining the stories of John the Baptist and Jesus, we do seem to be clearly in mythological territory. Their two stories reflect each other perfectly. They both have miraculous births. John is born to an old woman. Jesus is born to a young woman. John's mother is infertile. Jesus' mother is unfertilised. John is born at the summer solstice when the sun begins to wane. Jesus is born six months later at the winter solstice when the sun begins to wax again – hence the Baptist's declaration about Jesus: "He must grow greater, I must become less". John is born in the astrological sign of Cancer, which for the ancients represented the gate of the souls into incarnation. Jesus is born in the astrological sign of Capricorn, which for the ancients represented the gate of souls out of incarnation into immortality. John baptises with water and Jesus with fire and spirit. The birthday of Jesus is celebrated on the Pagan festival of the returning sun on 25 December. The birthday of John the Baptist is celebrated in June, replacing a Pagan midsummer festival of water.'
(Timothy Freke and Peter Gandy, *The Jesus Mysteries*)

We have already observed how the four Celtic treasures of sovereignty were absorbed into the mythology of Jesus as Winter King and John the Baptist as Summer King: spear and bowl to Jesus, sword and platter to John the Baptist. The mythology of the annual challenge between the Summer King and the Winter King is an old pattern told in many variations by many cultures and it is present in the Arthurian romances in many ways; always between two men fighting over a female personification of sovereignty.

THE WINTER KING verses THE SUMMER KING

The common folklore story of the Oak King of summer verses the Holly King of winter; usually to win union with the Queen of the May.

In British mythology the Winter King, Gwyn ap Nudd, fights the Summer King, Gwythyr ap Greidawl, every year at Beltaine, to win the hand of Creurdylad the goddess of spring. In the night sky Gwyn ap Nudd is the constellation of Orion (the Winter Hunter) and the Summer King's constellation is Orion's perpetual enemy, the constellation of Scorpius. They battle for all time until the day of doom.

Geoffrey of Monmouth, in his *History of the Kings of Britain* (1136) has King Arthur (the old king) being usurped by Mordred his nephew (the young king) who has kidnapped the queen of the land, Guinevere. In the *Welsh Triads* Guinevere is described as the daughter of Gwythyr ap Greidawl (the Summer King that fights Gwyn ap Nudd). In later romances the Round Table (which represents the cycle of the year) comes to Arthur as Guinevere's dowry when they marry.

Caradoc of Llancarfan, in his *Life of Gildas* (1155) tells the story of King Arthur taking his army to Glastonbury to rescue Queen Guinevere who had been kidnapped by Melvas, 'king of the summer country' (Summer King). Llancarfan says that Arthur,
'... searched for the queen throughout **the course of one year**...'
This was never literal history.

And there are many other variations of this theme. They are pre-Christian wisdom stories written into medieval romance; salvaged at a time when anything heretical was being erased.

* * *

Both Glastonbury and Vézelay have very curious winter solstice and summer solstice intrigues. The windows of Vézelay Abbey are positioned in such a way that every year, at summer solstice, the central nave of the abbey is illuminated by the midday sun (see the photo on page 103).

This wonderful phenomenon predates Vézelay's Mary Magdalene tradition and it probably implies that the site had some special affinity with the cult of John the Baptist long before it became the cult centre for the Magdalene; maybe Les Fontaines Salées had been used for rites of baptism?

Glastonbury Tor has a wonderfully unique winter solstice phenomenon. From an old mound on a neighbouring hill, every year at the winter solstice sunrise (weather permitting), the sun can be seen to roll perfectly up Glastonbury Tor to its very summit. Furthermore, it would have been seen to enter the Romano-British temple that stood upon the Tor before the church of Saint Michael was put there.

Vézelay and Glastonbury, two very important Benedictine abbeys. Both situated upon pilgrimage routes to the furthest west, both in Avalon, and one significant to the winter solstice and the other significant to the summer solstice. Both wrapped up with the Angevin Empire and the creation of the Arthurian romances. Both a part of larger Earth Mysteries intrigues.

* * *

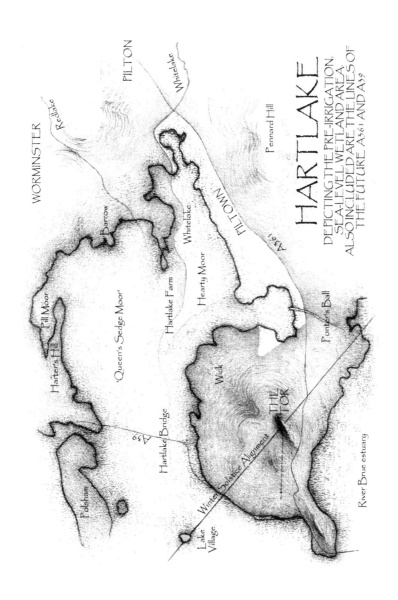

HARTLAKE

DEPICTING THE PRE-IRRIGATION
SEA LEVEL WETLAND AREA.
ALSO INCLUDED ARE THE LINES OF
THE FUTURE A361 AND A39

WORMINSTER

PILTON

Redlake

Whitelake

Barrow

PILTOWN

A361

Whitelake

Pennard Hill

Pill Moor

Harter's Hill

'Queen's Sedge Moor'

Hartlake Farm

Hearty Moor

Ponter's Ball

Palsham

Hartlake Bridge

A39

Wick

THE TOR

Winter Solstice Alignment

Lake Village.

River Brue estuary

SCS
HVGO
EP

LIN
COLN

APPENDIX III
SAINT HUGH OF AVALON

Many years ago, whilst investigating the history of King Arthur's grave at Glastonbury, I was reading a rather dull and boring book, *Henry II* by W. L. Warren; it was scholarly, academic, and needlessly tedious. Much to my surprise my boredom turned into fascination when I came across a reference to one Hugh of Avalon. Two years after the Great Fire of Glastonbury Abbey (which happened in 1184)...

'In 1186 Henry pressed upon Hugh of Avalon the bishopric of Lincoln, (and paid the cost of the consecration ceremony). Indeed he conceived such an affection for the saintly Hugh and accepted rebukes from him with such good grace that there were many who were convinced that Hugh must be the king's natural son.'
(W.L. Warren, *Henry II*)

The above quote astounded me for a number of reasons; not in the least that Hugh of Avalon may have been an illegitimate half-brother of Richard the Lionheart. Hugh of Avalon was active in Somerset itself long before the hoax of King Arthur's grave established Glastonbury as the true location of Avalon. Was Hugh from Glastonbury? No, of course he wasn't, he was from Burgundy.

Hugh of Avalon is now better known as Saint Hugh of Lincoln; and as that celebrated bishop he was quite well known. He was a religious obsessive but he had been brought up that way. His mother died when he was a young child and he was made to join a monastery at the vulnerable age of ten years old; to say that this badly effected his attitude towards women and the sins of the flesh would be a major understatement.

'But the life of an Augustinian did not suit Hugh. What

disturbed him was contact with the secular world which experience proved was all too likely to inflame a young man's sexual desire. A pretty girl who touched his arm with a 'gentle squeeze' caused Hugh to seize a sharp knife and cut out the portion of flesh which had been the object of the embrace. The author of the 'Metrical Life' tells us that 'by this means mad passion was overcome', but it did not represent a permanent solution. With temptation always just around the corner, Hugh decided to forsake society and seek solitude and deeper spiritual challenge amongst the Carthusians at La Grande Chartreuse.'
(David Marcombe, *The Saint and the Swan*)

As a devout bishop he did a very strange thing during one visit to France; he ate a piece of Mary Magdalene's arm; and he was admired for it.

'Hugh of Lincoln (d.1200), an avid collector of bones, who carried a silver casket containing countless fragments of saints of both sexes when consecrating churches, visited the monastery of Fécamp in northern France. Which owned an arm of Mary Magdalene. Desiring a bit for himself, he took the arm, with a knife unwrapped it from the cloths of silk and linen which were tightly bound round it, and which the monks had never dared open, and tried to break off a piece with his fingers. Finding it too hard, he then, to the shock and anger of the monks present, bit it first with his incisors, and finally attacked it with his molars. With charming logic, he justified his somewhat rude treatment of the holy remains with the following words: "If a little while ago I handled the most sacred body of the Lord of all the saints with my fingers, in spite of my unworthiness, and when I partook of it [during Communion], touched it with my lips and teeth, why should I not venture to treat in the same way the bones of the saints... and without profanity acquire them when I have the opportunity?"'
(Susan Haskins, *Mary Magdalene: Myth and Metaphor*)

The 12ᵗʰ century was a long time ago but surely munching mummified body parts is an odd thing to do in any era; but Hugh was highly respected. King John (who may even of been his half-brother), helped to carry Hugh's coffin at his funeral.

'If he had been archbishop of Canterbury or York he would probably have been as famous as St Wilfrid or St Thomas Becket. Unlike these two saints, however, he did not quarrel with kings. He opposed them, reproved them, criticised them, but he also made them laugh. The three kings whom he knew personally and whose affection he enjoyed were Angevins. Henry II, the powerful ruler who was partially responsible for Becket's death, chose Hugh for the see of Lincoln. Richard I, the crusader who neglected England, was reproached by Hugh for simony and infidelity. John, who lost Normandy to the French and after signing Magna Carta did feudal homage for England to the pope, carried Hugh's coffin at his funeral.'
(David Hugh Farmer, *Saint Hugh of Lincoln*)

My only real interest in Saint Hugh was that his original name was 'of Avalon' and that for more than fifteen years before the monks of Glastonbury invented King Arthur's grave (thereby establishing Glastonbury as Avalon) there was actually a 'Mr Avalon' active in Somerset and living just 17 miles east of Glastonbury.

As reparation for the death of Thomas Becket, Henry II founded a Charterhouse at Witham in Somerset. In 1175 Henry II had Hugh of Avalon (who may have been his illegitimate son) come to Somerset to be prior of Witham. In 1186 Henry II made him bishop of Lincoln, the largest diocese in England. Curiously, as bishop of Lincoln Hugh appointed Gerald of Wales as an archdeacon; the same Gerald of Wales that wrote the first account of King Arthur's grave at Glastonbury. Hugh died in the year 1200 and he was canonised by pope Honorius III in 1220.

Sir Pelleas

From the Well Maidens of the Summerlands project

www.wellmaidens.co.uk

APPENDIX IV
THE HIGH HISTORY OF THE HOLY GRAAL

Some time around the year 1220, *The High History of the Holy Graal* was written and within its pages it claimed to have been based upon a history that was kept at Glastonbury Abbey. In its final pages it stated that,

'The Latin from whence this history was drawn into romance was taken in the Isle of Avalon, in the holy house of religion that standeth at the head of the Moors Adventurous, there where King Arthur and Queen Guenievre lie, according to the witness of the good men religious that are therein, that have the whole history thereof, true from the beginning even to the end.'
(The High History of the Holy Graal)

Whilst Glastonbury is not specifically mentioned, no other '*holy house of religion*' claims to have the bodies of Arthur and Guinevere; or to be the Isle of Avalon. One of the most enigmatic things about the above quote is that it describes Glastonbury as being situated '*at the head of the Moors Adventurous*' and this is really very important.

The Moors Adventurous is an actual location within the story of the *High History of the Holy Graal* and so the implication is that the places in the *High History* are actually real world locations.

By careful study of the *High History* and by looking at maps of Somerset, one could back-step from Glastonbury and the Somerset Levels (the Moors Adventurous) and plot out the rest of the locations described in the Grail romance. A lady called Katharine Maltwood undertook this very challenge and throughout the 1920s she came to believe that she had successfully figured out the geographical locations of the adventures of King Arthur and his knights.

In 1929 Katharine Maltwood persuaded the publishers, J.M. Dent & Sons, to print detailed maps of her Arthurian landscape and attach them into their latest print run of *The High History of the Holy Graal.* The title on Katharine's map was,

Map to the
High History of the Holy Graal.
The Kingdom of
Logres and the Round Table.

Katharine's map was black and white but with Arthurian place-names printed in bright red ink. There are too many locations to describe but here are a few:

'**The Castle of Joy**' is near the village of Baltonsborough.
'**The Castle of Griffins**' is near Kingweston.
'**Burning Castle**' in the '**Wearisome Forest**' is Brent Knoll.
King Arthur's castle of '**Cardoil**' is Caerleon-upon-Usk.
Wearyall Hill, Glastonbury, is the '**Fisherman's Castle**',
and so on.

Curiously, a major section of her map has two large bright red, slightly over-lapping, circles drawn upon it (presumably corresponding with the the 'Round Table' in the map's title). One circle has *EQUATOR* written upon it and the other circle has *ECLIPTIC* written upon it. The circles cover quite a large area of Somerset. In the north is Glastonbury (and in red, **Isle of Avalon**) and in the south is Somerton (with **Lord of the Moors** written in red). Near Somerton, and between the Equator and the Ecliptic, in bright red ink, is the word **LEO**. The words Ecliptic and Leo can only mean one thing and that is the circle of the signs of the zodiac; furthermore, directly opposite **LEO** is Glastonbury which therefore corresponds **Isle of Avalon** with the sign of Aquarius. Why would any of this zodiacal information be on an Arthurian adventure map?

We have already observed (on page 56) that the Round

Table itself often did represent the circle of the zodiac and the heavenly kingdom. At the beginning of the *High History of the Holy Graal* it describes the knights of the Round Table as numbering three-hundred and sixty-sixty which is equal to a 'year and a day'; a year is not 365 days but is actually 365.25 days, which is why we have a Leap Year every four years. If there were 366 knights of the Round Table then there must have been 366 seats at the Round Table; or rather, the Round Table in the *High History* represented the passage of Time through one cycle of the zodiac.

Thus, since before the middle of the 13th century it was established that King Arthur's Round Table represented the wheel of the year and also the stars, constellations and planets of the night sky. If the Round Table represented the heavens and the passage of time then the knights that sat around it represented something much more than human; they represented mythic culture heroes whose adventures and quests would be played out at their allotted time.

Katharine Maltwood may have begun her Arthurian quest by looking for adventure locations by back-stepping from the Moors Adventurous but she soon found herself walking among the stars. She came to believe that the *High History* was an encoded story-book that described a vast terrestrial star map. Some six years after her map was printed into the back of copies of the *High History* she published her own book revealing her entire Arthurian zodiac, *The Guide to Glastonbury's Temple of the Stars*. Katharine's book was published in 1935 and it was packed full with many obscure quotes from *The High History of the Holy Graal*.

Katharine Maltwood's ideas are very esoteric and obscure. She was well-versed in ancient Mystery Tradition lore and one can clearly see that she was promoting a revival of the Arthurian Mysteries. As controversial as her ideas may be, her work drove her on to studying the star-lore of many ancient religions and mythologies; and it is for her acquired knowledge of star-lore that her writings are most valuable. Her Temple of the Stars is now better known as the 'Glastonbury Zodiac' and it is one of Glastonbury's most enigmatic and controversial visitor attractions.

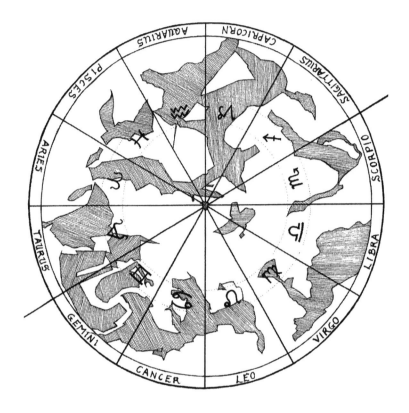

The Temple of the Stars.
'The Glastonbury Zodiac'
is a key to certain Arthurian star-lore Mysteries.

For further information about Katharine Maltwood and other landscape mysteries around Glastonbury, please see my book, *The Terrestrial Alignments of Katharine Maltwood and Dion Fortune*. The image on the opposite page is a glimpse into the complexities of Katharine's *High History* star-lore in relation to her *Temple of the Stars*.

ARTHURIAN CHARACTERS FROM THE 'HIGH HISTORY'
AND THEIR POSITIONS ON THE ZODIAC
ACCORDING TO KATHARINE MALTWOOD

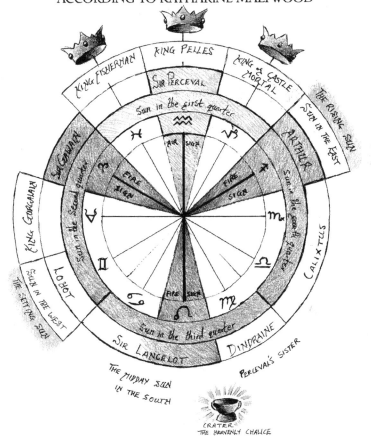

The Ruins of Glastonbury Abbey

THE 'ORRIBLE HISTORY OF GLASTONBURY ABBEY
(This Appendix could also be called, The Bloody Abbey, or more
kindly, A History of Unrest in the Holy House of God.)

There is a romantic tendency in Glastonbury to look
upon the ruins of the abbey and to imagine its previous
glory as being pure and spiritually profound but this is far
from the historical truth. Whilst individual monks may
have joined to live devout and sincere lives many of the
abbots were simply greedy noblemen looking to reap wealth
and power for themselves. What follows is a brief glimpse
of some of the less than holy highlights of the abbey's
darker history. Most of this information comes from the
very scholarly, *Glastonbury Abbey: The Holy House at the
Head of the Moors Adventurous,* by James P. Carley; and
The Antiquities of Glastonbury, translated by Frank Lomax.

Abbot Aethelweard
mutilated the dead, went insane, then broke his neck.
Aethelweard was one of the last Saxon abbots of
Glastonbury; his abbacy was between 1024 and 1053 AD.

*'Aethelweard, we are told, decided to excavate King Edgar's tomb
and found the body miraculously preserved. Rather than being
moved to devotion by this discovery, however, he proceeded to
hack the body up in order to make it fit into the reliquary he had
provided for it. In response to this violation the body began to
bleed profusely and Aethelweard, in turn, became incurably
insane. Not long afterwards he fell as he left the church and
broke his neck.'*
(James P. Carley, *Glastonbury Abbey*)

Abbot Thurstan
had his own monks killed at the high altar because they would not sing the way that he wanted them to.
Thurstan was the first of the Norman abbots of
Glastonbury; his abbacy was between 1077 and 1096 AD.

He did not like the Gregorian chanting that the monks of Glastonbury used to sing their devotions and he insisted that they sing in a new style (that which was created by William of Féchamp) but the monks refused to adapt to the new style and so Thurstan lost his temper in a huge way:

'When therefore he once entered the monastery, a storm raging within him, and addressed the monks concerning these and other matters in turbulent fashion without being able to bend them to his will, blinded with sudden anger, he had his soldiers and his bowmen summoned. When they saw this, the monks, seized with extreme fear, took flight as best they could, and sought asylum in the church, whose threshold they barricaded. But the servants of Belial, bursting into the temple, showed extraordinary wickedness, and pursued the monks, as they fled, right up to the very altar, where they implored the Divine help, with tears flowing down. Nay, the ruffians mounted the triforium galleries erected between the columns, in order that they might the more readily glut their evil mind with innocent blood. Neither reverence for the place nor for the saints there could hinder them from transfixing with a lance one of the monks, who had embraced the altar, and killing another, also at the altar's edge, with an arrow, to say nothing of seriously wounding fourteen more. The monks then, pressed by such necessity, began to defend themselves as well as they were able, and thrust their opponents from the choir; but one of the abbot's retainers, bolder in his wickedness than the rest, perceiving one of the monks, holding the aforesaid cross, covered with silver, in his hand, in order that it might serve him for a shield, shot an arrow towards it in a contemptuous spirit, but, by the providence of God, the arrow wounded the Image of the Lord, fixed in the cross, below the knee, and caused a rivulet of blood to flow therefrom, which,descending from the altar to the steps, from the steps to the ground, struck the unhappy men with a terror of Divine vengeance. At sight of this, the perpetrator of the crime, unable to bear his confusion, immediately lost his senses, and, after he got outside the church, he fell to the ground, fractured his skull, and died.'
(The Antiquities of Glastonbury)

The king of England, William the Conqueror, on learning of the above outrage, sent Thurstan back to Normandy and all of the wounded monks to other monasteries to recover and start lives anew.

Abbot Seffrid Pelochin
was a devotee of the serpent god Abraxas

Seffrid Pelochin was not so much a bad abbot, but rather an enigmatically controversial one; his abbacy was short-lived, between 1120 and 1125 AD.

'Seffride's allegiance to Glastonbury, however, does not appear to have been absolute and in 1125 he left to become bishop of Chichester, from which position he was deposed in 1145 on the grounds of sodomy. He was buried at Chichester; many centuries later his coffin was opened and it was discovered that his episcopal ring was made of jasper and was carved with the gnostic figure of the serpent god Abraxas. His ring is still on display at Chichester Cathedral. In the Middle Ages, gnosticism was often associated with homosexuality – as the derivation of 'buggar' from 'Bulgar' and the suppression of the Templars suggest – and Seffrid's ring could indicate that his crimes might concern his religious beliefs rather than his sexual preferences. If – as can no way be proved – his putative interest in gnosticism were to date from his time at Glastonbury, then this might in turn throw some light on the seemingly gnostic hints in William of Malmesbury's reference to the mysterious pattern of triangles and squares on the pavement of the church at Glastonbury; "There [in the Old Church] one can observe all over the floor stones, artfully interlaced in the forms of triangles or squares and sealed with lead; I do no harm to religion if I believe some sacred mystery is contained beneath them."'
(James P. Carley, *Glastonbury Abbey*)

To shed some light upon the nature of Gnosticism and the god Abraxas we can turn to *The Encyclopedia of the Occult* by Lewis Spence:

*'**Abraxas**: (or Abracax). The Basilidian sect of Gnostics, of the second century, claimed Abraxas as their supreme god, and said that Jesus Christ was only a phantom sent to earth by him. They believed that his name contained great mysteries as it was composed of the seven Greek letters which form the number 365,*

which is also the number of days in a year. Abraxas, they thought, had under his command 365 gods, to whom they attributed 365 virtues, one for each day. The older Mythologists placed him among the number of Egyptian gods, and demonologists have described him as a demon, with the head of a king and with serpents forming his feet. He is represented on ancient amulets, with whip in hand. It is from his name that the mystic word, Abracadabra is taken. Many stones and gems cut in various symbolic forms, such as the head of a fowl, a serpent, and so forth, were worn by Basilidians as amulets.'

If James Carley is correct, that the unusual floor of interlaced triangles and squares inside Glastonbury's Old Church was Gnostic in origin, then it probably represented the cycle of the year in some manner; the most common way to do this would be to use the signs of the zodiac or some other astronomical geometric design. The floor design must have been quite unusual for William of Malmesbury to be so awkwardly cautious about it.

Abbot Henry of Blois
opportunistic good guy or bad guy?
His abbacy was between 1126 and 1171 AD.

As we have already seen (on page 24) whether Henry of Blois was a good guy or a bad guy depended upon which side you were on, during the early civil war, The Anarchy:

*St. Bernard of Clairvaux contemptuously labelled him variously a rival pope, the old wizard of Winchester, and the whore of Winchester. Even with, or perhaps as a result of, his redoubtable administrative abilities and royal connections he managed to get himself embroiled in complex and sometimes **unsavory political intrigues** and on occasion **military skirmishes**.*
(James P. Carley, *Glastonbury Abbey*)

Regardless of 12th century political spin; how do we judge Henry of Blois? Do we really believe that he just happened to find Saint David's Sapphire Altar, and adorn it with precious jewels for pilgrims to admire, the very year after the Pope had made David a saint of the Catholic church?

Henry of Blois was abbot of Glastonbury until he died; making his duration (of forty-five years) one of the longest in the abbey's history. The abbot that followed him (Robert of Winchester) was only abbot for seven years; during his abbacy began the long and uninspiring dispute with Wells cathedral over territories and land rights – houses of God squabbling over wealth. When Robert of Winchester died in 1180 the king, Henry II, did not allow Glastonbury to elect a new abbot; which was the king's right and allowed him to use Glastonbury's revenue for his own purposes (mainly to finance his wars in France). Henry II set his own man, Peter de Marcy, to running the affairs of Glastonbury Abbey and the power quite went to de Marcy's head.

Peter de Marcy
irreligion, the Great Fire, and divine punishment
1180 and 1184 AD.

The role of being the abbot of Glastonbury was a very important and lucrative position. Henry II's man, once in Glastonbury, attempted to become the new abbot but he was not at all popular with the monks of the abbey.

'Peter tried to persuade the monks to elect him as abbot, but they had heard rumours that he was irreligious, that he had a tendency to divert church funds to his own ends and that he had perhaps even engaged in mortal combat while bearing arms. To beguile the monks Peter 'feigned' a celebration of the Mass in the Old Church at Christmas. From the perspective of the community, this constituted a sacrilege since Peter was in a state of mortal sin at the time, and the church therefore stood in need of reconsecration. The evil was not, however, expiated in time and this accounted, so the chroniclers thought, for the next calamity which befell the monastery: on St Urban's Day (May 25th) 1184, a horrendous fire destroyed all the buildings except a chamber and chapel recently built by Robert and a bell tower built by Henry of Blois.'
(James P. Carly, *Glastonbury Abbey*)

The sacred Old Church was completely destroyed and the two Saxon crosses (the two tall 'pyramids') then became the oldest surviving structures of Glastonbury's antiquity.

'Gone was the beautiful Norman church, gone were the fine monastic buildings, Ine's church, the treasured vestments, ornaments, relic collections and books bequeathed by so many abbots and kings, and – most important of all – gone was the Old Church itself, universally hallowed as the first Christian church in Britain. (that it had been preserved after the Conquest and the resulting ecclesiastical building spree throughout England shows that it must have been perceived almost as a relic itself.) The consolation for the monks was that the wicked Peter de Marcy died soon afterwards.'
(James P. Carly, *Glastonbury Abbey*)

Ralph Fitzstephen
the rebuilding of the abbey and a great big lie
1184 to 1189 AD.

Ralph Fitzstephen was not an abbot he was another of Henry II's men but under the king's authority he acted as an abbot ('*in loco abbatis*') and Henry II allowed him to use all of the abbey's revenue to finance its restoration. Ralph Fitzstephen worked hard and the abbey was pretty much restored within two years. He managed to salvage some important relics from the burnt remains of the Old Church; relics of St Patrick, St Indract, and St Gildas. At least, that is what Fitzstephen claimed. The abbey desperately needed something to attract pilgrims to visit. Glastonbury's most famous abbot had been Saint Dunstan and, ta-da, Ralph just happened to discover the grave of Saint Dunstan; which centuries later was proven to be a complete lie.

'Even more remarkable was the discovery of St Dunstan's bones which – so it transpired – had long been secretly hidden in the church. This new discovery, not surprisingly, sparked a bitter controversy with the monks of Christ Church Canterbury, who also claimed to possess Dunstan's remains.'
(James P. Carly, *Glastonbury Abbey*)

*'DUNSTAN: - Canterbury possessed his body, though
Glastonbury too claimed it: the controversy was only finally
settled when the Canterbury tomb was opened in 1508.'*
(David Hugh Farmer, *The Oxford Dictionary of Saints*)

In 1189 Henry II died and so too did his man in
Glastonbury. With Ralph Fitzstephen and his supposed
discovery of Saint Dunstan's grave a precedent had been
established for falsehood; but Dunstan (an old Saxon saint)
was just not sexy enough so a bigger attraction was needed.

Henry of Sully
and the King Arthur's grave hoax
His abbacy was between 1189 and 1193 AD.

*'The new king, Richard I, was concerned with crusading and had
none of his predecessor's interest in Glastonbury; construction,
as John of Glastonbury would later observe, 'therefore ceased,
since there was no one to give the labourers their wages.'
Richard appointed his own nephew Henry of Sully (1189-93)
as abbot.'*
(James P. Carly, *Glastonbury Abbey*)

As soon as the publicity of King Arthur's grave had been
established (by Gerald of Wales in 1193) Henry of Sully quit
Glastonbury and basically did a runner (see page 38).

Savaric Fitzgeldewin
the monk-torturing bishop of Bath and Glastonbury
His abbacy was between 1193 and 1205 AD.

*'In the next abbot Savaric Fitzgeldewin (1193-1205) Glastonbury
did acquire a wolfish master, one whose personal ambition knew
no bounds and who saw Glastonbury Abbey as a pawn in his own
political game.'*
(James P. Carly, *Glastonbury Abbey*)

Savaric was a battle-hardened crusader and he had
accompanied Richard the Lionheart on the Third Crusade
which means that he most likely knew Philip the Count of

Flanders (the patron that had commissioned Chrétien de Troyes to write the story about the Graal). Savaric became bishop of Bath in August 1192 whilst Richard's nephew was still abbot of Glastonbury.

'In the meantime, King Richard had been captured by Savaric's relation the German emperor Henry VI, and Savaric was appointed to act as intermediary in arranging the terms for his release. Now in a position of even greater strength than before... ...Savaric had insisted that Richard agree to an annexation of Glastonbury to the See of Bath.'
(James P. Carly, *Glastonbury Abbey*)

So Savaric became the bishop of Bath and Glastonbury; which entitled him to a huge amount of wealth and power. Once he had been freed from captivity King Richard I regretted giving Glastonbury to the see of Bath (he wanted its wealth for himself of course) and he allowed the monks of Glastonbury to ignore bishop Savaric and to elect a new abbot for themselves; they elected William Pica and he became abbot of Glastonbury on November 25, 1198.

'Savaric was predictably furious and excommunicated William and his supporters.'
(James P. Carly, *Glastonbury Abbey*)

Glastonbury's chosen abbot, William Pica, had to travel to Rome, to visit the pope, to get the excommunication cleared.

'While Pica was in Rome Richard died and was succeeded by King John, whom Savaric won over to his point of view (through substantial bribes, according to the chroniclers). Seeing himself in a position of strength again, Savaric decided that it was now time to take Glastonbury by force and he came with a band of armed men to the monastery where he had the gates forced open. He then marched in and had himself enthroned as abbot. Those of the monks who would not submit to him were dragged out into the courtyard and severely beaten. They were then locked in the infirmary, deprived of food and water and tortured in various

other ways. Indeed, the treatment was so harsh that at least one monk died of his wounds.
(James P. Carly, *Glastonbury Abbey*)

Even after the above brutal enforcement many of the monks of Glastonbury continued to complain about their abbey belonging to the see of Bath.

'Soon the resistance became so intense that one Jocelyn of Wells – later to be bishop of Bath – came back to the monastery with a troop of soldiers, laymen rather than monks. This band arrived just as the monks were about to celebrate High Mass. They pushed their way into the church and dragged off the five strongest protesters, one 'per virilia' and put them in prison in Wells where, after cruel punishments, they were deported to other monasteries.'
(James P. Carly, *Glastonbury Abbey*)

'...William Pica [the monks own choice of abbot] *died mysteriously in Rome and the monks suspected that he had been poisoned by Savaric's agents. They sent new monks to Rome, but in every case these individuals were waylaid by Savaric's men. The situation seemed to grow more oppressive and more hopeless practically by the day. At this dark hour, however, Savaric died suddenly...'*
(James P. Carly, *Glastonbury Abbey*)

Because of Savaric Fitzgeldewin's manipulations to make Glastonbury an annex of the see of Bath, many years of struggle followed between various bishops of Bath and abbots of Glastonbury; it all boiled down to squabbling over the ownership of land rights and the value of various estates and territories. Much of Glastonbury's vast estates were taken by Bath. It was during these arguments over land rights that an 'unknown hand' added the Joseph of Arimathea story of the Twelve Hides of land to *The Antiquities of Glastonbury*; successfully securing for all time that at least the said twelve areas of land remained with Glastonbury. King Henry III supported Glastonbury and the 'traditional liberty' of the Twelve Hides.

John of Taunton
earthquake, Longshanks, and Arthurian intrigues
His abbacy was between 1274 and 1291 AD.

John of Taunton was not an 'orrible abbot but the king of England during his abbacy was pretty brutal; Edward I, 'Longshanks' (who was infamously portrayed as the wicked nemesis of William Wallace in the film *Braveheart*) was a big King Arthur enthusiast.

A very curious thing happened during the second year of John of Taunton's abbacy; an earthquake destroyed the church of St Michael on top of Glastonbury Tor. Strangely, this happened on September 11th (1275) the same date as the destruction of the twin towers in America in recent history. Glastonbury was struggling to manage its finances (especially as so much land had been lost to the see of Bath) and now with the Tor church to rebuild it needed help. King Edward I stepped in and used King Arthur and Queen Guinevere's remains to his own advantage.

'King Edward had an even more powerful allegiance to Glastonbury because of its Arthurian associations. He saw his various military campaigns as Arthurian adventures and he cultivated an image of himself as 'Arthurus redivivus'. After his first victorious expedition into North Wales in 1277, Edward forced Llewelyn to do him homage and not long afterwards he claimed the crown of Arthur from the Welsh – a trophy which, unlike the Stone of Scone (another of his imperial trophies), was soon afterwards permanently lost. At Easter 1278 he and Queen Eleanor, accompanied by Robert Kilwardby, archbishop of Canterbury, came to Glastonbury to celebrate a major Arthurian event timed to coincide with the consecration of the High Altar...

...King Edward wrapped his illustrious predecessor's remains in a precious pall and Queen Eleanor did the same with Guinevere's, and the relics were placed in the chests, although the head and knee joints of each were temporarily kept out to be shown to the people to encourage their devotion. The caskets were finally reverently placed in a stately mausoleum before the High Altar,

that is, in the most appropriate position for a saintly founder's tomb. In this highly public ceremony Edward was clearly emphasizing that he was the legitimate successor to Arthur as king of all Britain.'
(James P. Carly, *Glastonbury Abbey*)

1267 ~ England recognised Llewelyn ap Gruffudd as the Prince of Wales.

1272 ~ Edward I became the king of England.

1275 ~ An earthquake destroyed the church on Glastonbury Tor.

1277 ~ Edward I went to Wales and forced Llewelyn to pay him homage (and claimed the crown of King Arthur)

1278 ~ Edward I and Queen Eleanor transferred the remains of King Arthur and Queen Guinevere to the High Altar of Glastonbury Abbey.

1283 ~ Llewelyn ap Gruffudd, the last true Prince of Wales, was killed and Edward I had his severed head put triumphantly on display in London.

1305 ~ William Wallace ('Braveheart') was captured and executed.

Nicholas Frome
and the 'tradition' of Joseph of Arimathea fail
His abbacy was between 1420 and 1456 AD.

Nicholas Frome was not a bad abbot but he had to suffer humiliation in Europe over Glastonbury's Joseph of Arimathea claim. He and his companions kept poker-faced about it all, and did not back down, but the Glastonbury 'tradition' was never taken seriously in Europe ever again.

'In 1434, acting as the chief representative of England's apostolic church, he attended the council of Basel and wrote a letter – preserved in a manuscript at Trinity College, Cambridge – describing his experiences. At the council the Castilian ambassador expressed extreme scepticism about Joseph of Arimathea's mission to Britain and challenged the English to prove that he ever really came. He also referred to a counter legend, recorded in the 'Golden Legend', which narrates that Joseph was not freed from prison until 70 AD, in which case he could not have come to England several years earlier [Glastonbury claimed 63 AD]. Although Frome and his fellow

English delegates stoutly maintained their position and continued
to uphold the Glastonbury tradition throughout the council,
Joseph's name would never come up again in the conciliar
context.'
(James P. Carly, *Glastonbury Abbey*)

Basel, the location of the above mentioned council, is in Switzerland on the west side of the Alps; not far from the 'Burgundy Gate' of Belfort – a natural route through the Alps that leads into the heart of Burgundy (due west of which stand Avallon and Vézelay).

Richard Beere
and the re-vamp of Joseph of Arimathea
His abbacy was between 1493 and 1524 AD.

During the abbacy of Richard Beere, the penultimate abbot of Glastonbury, the 'tradition' of Joseph of Arimathea was given a brand new make-over.

'Beere was fascinated by St Joseph of Arimathea to a greater
degree than any other abbot in Glastonbury's history...

...A variety of factors may have influenced Beere in his veneration
of Joseph. Certainly, the Arthurian legend was undergoing one of
its periodic revivals and Sir Thomas Malory had not long since
completed his Arthuriad; in his preface to the printed edition,
moreover, William Caxton underscored Glastonbury's Arthurian
connection...

...Mostly, however, he [Beere] seems to have been a natural
*entrepreneur and **Joseph constituted first-rate material for***
***exploitation**. Beere established a prominent shrine to St*
Joseph...

...Around 1502 an anonymous 'Life' of Joseph of Arimathea was
composed – which was then published in 1520 – and it refers
*specifically to St Joseph's Chapel (**as the newly dug out crypt***
under the Lady Chapel was now called)...
... In other words, under Beere's management, we at last see the

*appearance of a fully developed, **carefully orchestrated cult**
designed to attract pilgrims.*

*Beere also created an Arimathean coat of arms – a white shield
with drops of blood scattered over the white field and a central
green, knotted cross, flanked on either side by a golden ampoule.'*
(James P. Carly, *Glastonbury Abbey*)

In short then: Glastonbury's Joseph of Arimathea 'tradition' was invented in the 13th century; it was then justifiably ridiculed at the council of Basel in the 15th century; Abbot Richard Beere re-vamped the 'tradition' and created a St Joseph chapel in the 16th century (to create a 'carefully orchestrated cult'); and it was given fresh momentum in the 20th century with the wonderful stained-glass window of Joseph in St John's church, and the planting of the holy thorn on Wearyall Hill (see page 48).

Richard Whiting
the last abbot and the destruction of the abbey
His abbacy was between 1525 and 1539 AD.

In Europe, during the 1500s, there was a huge theological and political movement away from the Catholic Church and the political/religious power of the pope. Historically the Reformation began in Germany in 1517 under the leadership of Martin Luther. Non-Catholic Christians became known a Protestants (because they protested against Rome's control and interpretation of the Bible) and for the first time the Bible was printed into common languages (French, German, English etc) rather than the Latin used by the Vatican. People could thus read for themselves and think for themselves; and debate the contradictions of what the Bible actually did and did not say. Throughout the 1500s England became a religious battle-field between Protestants and Catholics; creating divisions that still effect some corners of the British Isles even to this very day (some five-hundred years later). Glastonbury Abbey came to an end due to the religious and political upheavals of the 1500s but it needn't have as not all abbeys and churches were destroyed; Tewkesbury Abbey, for instance, survived the turmoil and Glastonbury could have too but it chose not to co-operate.

Glastonbury was almost the wealthiest abbey in the land; it was second only to Westminster Abbey in London, and it was destroyed because the final abbot successfully concealed Glastonbury's vast wealth from the king of England. Tewkesbury Abbey, on the other hand, survived because the people of Tewkesbury chose to purchase their abbey from the king. Glastonbury was destroyed for no higher reason than that it refused to hand over its wealth; and it is still a mystery as to where all of the abbey's treasure was hidden.

1525 ~ Richard Whiting became the last abbot of Glastonbury.
1531 ~ Henry VIII became the head of the Church of England.
1534 ~ Henry VIII broke away from Rome and the Church of England became Protestant and independent.
1535 ~ Thomas Cromwell began to seize church wealth on behalf of the state; and the first Bible to be written in the English language was produced.
1539 ~ **The Dissolution of the Monasteries** was approved by Parliament. Abbot Whiting and two companions were hung on Glastonbury Tor.
1547 ~ Henry VIII died and his ten year old son became Edward VI; he was brought up to be a Protestant.
1553 ~ Edward VI died and his half-sister Mary Tudor became queen; she was a devout Catholic.
1555 ~ the **Persecution of the Protestants**; three-hundred people were executed and so the queen became known as Bloody Mary.
1558 ~ Mary Tudor died and her half-sister Elizabeth became queen; she was brought up to be a Protestant.
1559 ~ The Church of England was re-established.
1569 ~ Roman Catholic rebellion led by northern earls.
1587 ~ **Mary Queen of Scots was executed**.
1588 ~ Thirty-one Catholic priests were executed in England; and England was victorious against the Catholic **Spanish Armada**.

* * *

'O Glastonbury, Glastonbury:
The Threasory of the Carcasses of so famous,
and so many rare Persons...
How Lamentable, is thy case, now?
How hath Hypocrisie and Pride,
wrought thy Desolation?
Though I omit the names of very many other,
both excellent holy Men,
and Mighty Princes
(whose Carcasses are committed to thy Custody)
yet that Apostlelike Ioseph,
That Triumphant
BRYTISH ARTHUR,
and now,
this Peaceable, Provident SAXON,
King Edgar,
do force me,
with certain sorrowfull Reverence,
here,
to Celebrate thy Memory.'

(Dr John Dee, 1577, *The Perfect Art of Navigation*)

* * *

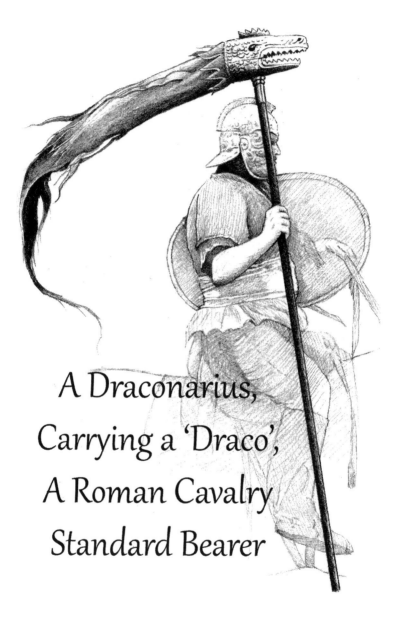

A Draconarius, Carrying a 'Draco', A Roman Cavalry Standard Bearer

Draco means Dragon.
A Dragon's head, in the British language,
is 'Pendragon'.

APPENDIX VI
THE HISTORICAL ARTHUR

There is very little evidence for the historical Arthur; as frustrating as that may be. There are just three scraps of information and the oldest does not mention him at all; just a battle (the Battle of Badon) which according to the two later scraps of information corresponded with Arthur. These three meagre pieces of evidence are,

Circa 540 AD ~ *The Ruin and Conquest of Britain*, by Gildas; describes the Battle of Badon as being a great victory for the Britons against the Saxons.

Circa 820 AD ~ *The History of the Britons*, by Nennius; gives the very first mention of Arthur. He is described as leading the kings of Britain through twelve battles and the most dynamic of which was the Battle of Badon (also a couple of 'wonders' are described which suggest that Arthur was mythical rather than historical).

Circa 970 AD ~ *The Welsh Annals*, list Arthur and the Battle of Badon; and also his death at the Battle of Camlann.

And that is all there really is.

There are many scattered place-names throughout the British Isles (like Arthur's Seat near Edinburgh) but it is impossible to know how old they may or may not be. There is a poem that is claimed to have been written by the 6th century bard, Aneirin, called the *Gododdin*, which simply has a passing statement about another warrior and describes him as being 'no Arthur' (implying that 'the Arthur' was truly great in deed). The oldest surviving copy of Aneirin's *Gododdin* was written long after the *Welsh Annals* and thus it is not possible to say that it was actually written in the 6th century.

According to the *Welsh Annals* the Battle of Badon

happened in the year 516 AD. Geoffrey of Monmouth's *History of the Kings of Britain* was the first biographical 'Life' of King Arthur and it was written about 1136 AD (six-hundred and twenty years after the Battle of Badon occurred) and Geoffrey's *History* is a work of fiction; although it is probably based upon British and Breton folk-stories which, although important, cannot by any stretch of the imagination be considered as historical. So, we must go back to the three original scraps of information.

GILDAS

'From then on victory went now to our country men, now to their enemies: so that in this people the Lord could make trial (as he tends to) of his latter-day Israel to see whether it loves him or not. This lasted right up till the year of the siege of Badon Hill, pretty well the last defeat of the villains, and certainly not the least.'
(*De Excidio Britonum*)

NENNIUS
(The Campaigns of Arthur)

'At that time the English increased their numbers and grew in Britain. On Hengist's death, his son Octha came down from the north of Britain to the kingdom of the Kentishmen, and from him are sprung the kings of the Kentishmen. Then Arthur fought against them in those days, together with the kings of the British; but he was their leader in battle.

The first battle was at the mouth of the river called Glein. The second, and third, the fourth, and the fifth were on another river, called the Douglas, which is in the country of Lindsey. The sixth battle was on the river called Bassas. The seventh battle was in Celyddon Forest, that is, the Battle of Celyddon Coed. The eight battle was in Guinnion fort, and in it Arthur carried the image of the holy Mary, the everlasting Virgin on his shield and the heathen were put to flight on that day, and there was a great slaughter upon them, through the power of Our Lord Jesus Christ and the power of the holy Virgin Mary, his mother. The ninth battle was fought in the city of the Legion. The tenth battle was fought on the bank of the river called Tryfrwyd. The eleventh battle was on the hill called Agned. The twelfth battle was on Badon Hill and in it nine hundred and sixty men fell in one day,

from a single charge of Arthur's, and no one laid them low save
he alone; and he was victorious in all his campaigns.
(*Historia Brittonum*)

WELSH ANNALS

'516 ~ The Battle of Badon, in which Arthur carried the Cross of
our Lord Jesus Christ for three days and three nights on his
shield and the Britons were the victors.
537 ~ The Battle of Camlann, in which Arthur and Medraut fell:
and there was plague in Britain and Ireland.
(*Annales Cambriae*)

There is a heavy influence of Christianity in all of these pieces of evidence; and that is because they were all written by Christian scribes. Arthur probably was a Celtic Christian because the Roman Empire had converted to Christianity in the 4th century and Arthur and his kin were Romano-Britons.

There are numerous books about the 'true' historical King Arthur and they all have to be based upon the above scraps of information because that is all there is. Most of the theories are based upon where the twelve battles may have taken place. The one constant in all three sources is the famous Battle of Badon:

Gildas calls is *Badonici montis*; 'Badon Hill'.
Nennius calls it *monte Badonis*; 'the Hill of Badon'.
The Welsh Annals call it *Bellum Badonis*; the Battle of Badon.

And where was the Battle of Badon? That is a very good question Sir Percival.

* * *

One can assume that the military techniques of the 6th century Dark Age Britons were very similar to those of their 5th century Romano-British ancestors. The picture on page 156 is an illustration of a Draconarius; the standard-bearer of the Roman cavalry throughout the empire. Wherever there was a unit of Roman cavalry (or dare we say 'knights') then there was also a dragon-headed battle-standard called a Draco (which is simply Latin for dragon); but more than this, Draco was (and still is) the biggest constellation at the centre of the night sky.

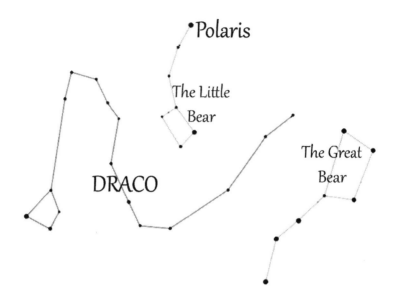

Roman culture represented the constellation of Draco the Dragon, and the two constellations of the Great Bear and the Little Bear, in a lovely stylised way; looking very much like the Chinese symbol of yin and yang. See the image at the top of the opposite page which is of the central detail of the Bianchini Tablet which is also shown below it. The Bianchini Tablet is a 3rd century Roman artefact and it depicts multiple zodiac wheels surrounded by the thirty-six spirits of the decans. This tablet, or round table, is an object of esoteric star-lore that is way beyond that of the common sun sign astrology that is to be found in modern newspapers and magazines.

Of interest right now is how Draco sits within the very centre of the night sky and that all of the other constellations circle around it; so too, in battle, the 'Pendragon' banner held the centre-point around which all of the other cavalry (knights) would gather as it raced across the battle-field (which, symbolically speaking, made the other knights represent the surrounding constellations).

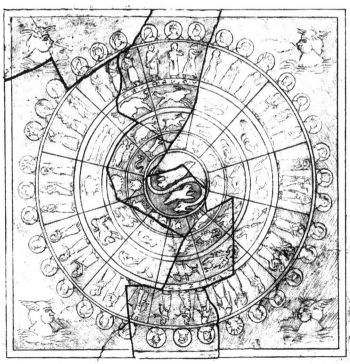

It is most probable that the Dark Age Britons (Arthur and his followers) continued to use the Draco battle-standard for their mounted warriors (and had knowledge of the star-lore that it represented). Even as late as the Norman invasion of England the Bretons had continued to use a Draco with their cavalry; as is clearly depicted upon the Bayeaux Tapestry.

A popular theory amongst many Arthurian scholars is that 'Arthur' was not actually the name of a specific individual but rather it was a title of honour given to a great battle-leader; and that it meant something like 'the Great Bear' (or more literally, the 'Long Bear', as in being tall and thus towering above all other men on the battle-field). If this is true then there would have been many Arthurs (many heroic battle-leaders) and this may explain why there are so many Arthur place-names across the British Isles (and also why Aneirin's *Gododdin* described one warrior as being 'no Arthur', that is, he was brave but the individual was no leader of men). It is within this strain of logic that Geoffrey Ashe suggested that Riothamus was 'the' Arthur that ended his days in Avallon, Burgundy, and why I have pointed out that Riothamus lived too early to have been 'the' Arthur at the Battle of Badon; but they could have both been influential elements upon the Arthur of legend and the French/Breton folk-memory that inspired Geoffrey of Monmouth's *History of the Kings of Britain*.

Although Draco the Dragon is the largest constellation in the centre of the night sky it is not the most visible; it is Ursa Major, the 'Great Bear' (also known as The Plough, and The Big Dipper) that visually dominates the central area of the northern hemisphere sky. Arthur's full medieval romantic name, Arthur Pendragon, incorporates both Draco and the Great Bear; and his Round Table, the stars that surround him (as already explained on page 56).

The *Historia Brittonum* of Nennius also describes a list of miraculous wonders (strange paranormal phenomena of the land itself); two of which relate to the 'warrior Arthur'.

'There is another wonder in the country called Builth. There is a heap of stones there, and one of the stones placed on top of the pile has the foot-print of a dog on it. When he hunted Twrch Trwyth Cafal, the warrior Arthur's hound, impressed his footprint on the stone, and Arthur later brought together the pile of stones, under the stone in which was his dog's footprint, and called it Carn Cafal. Men come and take the stone in their hands for the space of a day and a night, and on the morrow it is found upon the stone pile.

'There is another wonder in the country called Ergyng. There is a tomb there by a spring, called Llygad Amr; the name of the man who is buried in the tomb was Amr. He was a son of the warrior Arthur, and he killed him there and buried him. Men come to measure the tomb, and it is sometimes six feet long, sometimes nine, sometimes twelve, sometimes fifteen. At whatever measure you measure it on one occasion, you never find it again of the same measure, and I have tried it myself.'
(Nennius)

Both 'wonders' relate to mysterious and otherworldly phenomena. The first wonder mentions the hunt for Twrch Trwyth; which is a purely mythical wild boar that Arthur, accompanied by many British deities, has to capture (the story of which is told in the tale of *Kilhwch and Olwen* in *The Mabinogion*). The great hunt for Twrch Trwyth is the British mythological equivalent of the classical story from ancient Greece of the hunt for the Calydonian Boar; that was undertaken by many heroes and gods like Theseus and Hercules.

The two wonders described above, of the 'warrior Arthur', are clearly more mythic than representative of mundane human activity. There may have been a human Arthur at Avallon in Burgundy, and there may have been a human Arthur at the Battle of Badon, but the 'Warrior Great Bear' seems to have been something far more than a mortal man.

A mosaic of Helios the sun god
riding a chariot pulled by four horses
surrounded by the twelve signs of the zodiac.

APPENDIX VII
ARTHUR THE DEITY

About two-thousand and sixty years ago, Julius Caesar described the Celtic druids as being great astronomers.

*'A lesson which they take particular pains to inculcate is that the soul does not perish, but after death passes from one body to another; they think that this is the best incentive to bravery, because it teaches men to disregard the terrors of death. **They also hold long discussions about the heavenly bodies and their movements, the size of the universe and of the earth, the physical constitution of the world, and the power and properties of the gods**; and they instruct the young men in all these subjects.'*
(Julius Caesar, *The Conquest of Gaul*)

Originally, the druids refused to put their spiritual beliefs and teachings down in writing; their knowledge was kept intact by memory alone. If writing was not to be used then the best way of retaining information was by stories, poems, and songs. This special process of teaching the younger generations of druids astronomy, cosmology, and Celtic spirituality, through songs and stories, is the obvious origin of Celtic star-lore. The medieval Arthurian romances are an esoteric echo of the indigenous Celtic culture stories of western Europe; re-written by both orthodox and heretical Christian writers. By the time the medieval stories were written down the indigenous Celtic stories had also been influenced by the mythologies of the classical Mystery Traditions of the Roman Empire. That which unites all of the countries and cultures of the northern hemisphere is that they all share the same star constellations at night; the same celestial spirits shine down on every land. The 'heavenly kingdom' of the stars was divided into twelve sections many thousands of years ago; these twelve sections are called the signs of the zodiac. The **signs** of the zodiac actually measure the entire night sky not just the cluster-areas of the twelve zodiac **constellations**.

Mithras
surrounded by the signs of the zodiac.

'Jesus surrounds himself with 12 disciples. This is usually taken to be symbolic of the 12 tribes of Israel. This notion of 12 tribes, however, is itself a symbolic reference to the 12 signs of the zodiac in Babylonian astrology, which the Jews adopted whilst in exile in Babylon. The zodiac was an extremely important symbol in the Pagan world. Osiris-Dionysus is symbolically represented as the still spiritual centre of the turning wheel of change represented by the 12 signs. As Mithras, Dionysus, Aion and Helios, he is often depicted at the centre of the circling zodiac. During the initiation ceremony in the Mysteries of Mithras 12 disciples surrounded the godman, just as 12 disciples surrounded Jesus. The Mithraic disciples were dressed up to represent the 12 signs of the zodiac and circled the initiate, who represented Mithras himself.'
(Timothy Freke & Peter Gandy, *The Jesus Mysteries*)

Hercules, the great heroic sun god of the ancient world is primarily known for his many adventures achieving the impossible. The '**Twelve Labours** of Hercules' represent the journey of the sun as it passes through each of the twelve signs of the zodiac. In the very first writing that mentions Arthur (the *Historia Brittonum* by Nennius) our great hero is described as having achieved heroic victory through **twelve battles**; and the same book also describes two 'wonders' of the warrior Arthur that are truly mythic in essence. Is the earliest evidence really about a flesh and blood man or is it about something other? We are told that his main enemies were the Saxons but the *Anglo-Saxon Chronicles* make no mention of a British leader called Arthur; he is simply not on their radar (and you would have thought that they would have remembered a British leader that could kill more than nine-hundred Saxons, single-handedly, in just one charge).

The most well known Arthurian stories, for the most part, were written by French, Breton, and German writers. The more indigenous British, so-called 'Welsh', stories about Arthur are much more obscure and alien to modern readers with preconceived ideas; with difficult names to pronounce and stories jagged, garbled, and surreal. That said, it is quite clear that in the Welsh material Arthur was always something much more than a mere human being.

'The 'Coming of Arthur', his sudden rise into prominence, is one of the many problems of the Celtic mythology...

*... we find him lifted to the extraordinary position of a **king of gods**, to whom the old divine families of Dôn, of Llyr, and of Pwyll pay unquestioned homage. Triads tell us that Lludd – the Zeus of the older pantheon – was one of Arthur's 'Three Chief War-Knights', and Arawn, King of Hades, one of his 'Three Chief Counselling Knights'. In the story called the 'Dream of Rhonabwy', in the Red Book of Hergest, he is shown as a leader to whom are subject those we know to have been of divine race – sons of Nudd, of Llyr, of Brân, of Govannan, and of Arianrod. In another 'Red Book' tale, that of 'Kulhwch and Olwen', even greater gods are his vassals. Amaethon son of Dôn, ploughs for him, and Govannan son of Dôn, rids the iron, while two other sons of Beli, Nynniaw and Peibaw, 'turned into oxen on account of their sins', toil at the yoke, that a mountain may be cleared and tilled and the harvest reaped in one day. He assembles his champions to seek the 'treasures of Britain'; and Manawyddan son of Llyr, Gwyn son of Nudd, and Pryderi son of Pwyll rally around him at his call.'*
(Charles Squire, *Celtic Myth & Legend*)

This is not a book about the historical Arthur and neither is it a book about Arthur the deity, but there is enough shown in this humble appendix to completely dismiss the claim of King Arthur's grave in Glastonbury. How can a king of gods be buried?

"So Arthur is sometimes thought to be in Avilion, and sometimes to be sitting with his champions in a charmed sleep in some secret place, waiting for the trumpet to be blown that shall call him forth to reconquer Britain. The legend is found in the Eildon Hills; in the Snowdon district; at Cadbury, in Somerset, the best authenticated Camelot; in the Vale of Neath, in South Wales; as well as in other places. He slumbers, but he has not died. The ancient Welsh poem called "The Verses of the Graves of the Warriors" enumerates the last resting-places of most of the

*British gods and demi-gods. "The grave of Gwydion is in the
marsh of Dinlleu", the grave of Lleu Llaw Gyffes is "under the
protection of the sea with which he was familiar", and "where the
wave makes a sullen sound is the grave of Dylan"; we know the
graves of Pryderi, of Gwalchmei, of March, of Mabon, even the
great Beli, but, "Not wise the thought - a grave for Arthur"."*
(Charles Squire, *Celtic Myth and Legend*)

We observed on page 80 that according to the writings of
Chrétien de Troyes, King Arthur was Morgan le Fay's
brother. As Morgan is clearly more goddess than human
then so too must her brother be more divine than mortal.
Morgan probably evolved from Morrigan, the Great Queen,
and with her brother 'the Great Bear' (the celestial king of
the gods) they are more akin to the divine siblings of Egypt,
Isis and Osiris, than they are to any 6th century human
beings.

The name of Arthur's queen, Guinevere, is also
otherworldly and it translates as something like 'White
Ghost' or 'White Spirit'; making her akin to the White Lady
that haunts many forlorn landscapes or the White Goddess
of the Faerie Realm. More curious too is that in the Welsh
tradition Arthur actually had three queens and each was
called Guinevere (or rather, Gwenhwyfar in the Welsh
language): From the *Welsh Triads*,

'Arthur's Three Great Queens

*Gwenhwyfar daughter of Cywryd Gwent,
and Gwenhwyfar daughter of Gwythyr ap Greidiawl,
and Gwenhwyfar daughter of Gogfran the Giant.'*
(*Triad 56*)

Three 'White Spirits'; or rather, a Celtic triple goddess of
sovereignty and Light. The second Gwenhwyfar in the
Triad above is the daughter of the Summer King, Gwythyr
ap Greidiawl, that battles against the Winter King, Gwyn ap
Nudd, every Beltaine until the day of doom; do we really

believe that she was buried with Arthur in the graveyard of Glastonbury abbey; her limp blonde hair to be fondled by monks?

Arthur's most questionable grave at Glastonbury is the only evidence that Glastonbury is Avalon. But what is Avalon really? It is just a word from the medieval Latin and French romances. People have tried to find evidence of it in the indigenous Welsh stories; there is a poem in the *Black Book of Carmarthen* called *Yr Afallennau* (which simply means 'Apple-trees') and there is a demi-god called Avallach but neither of these correspond with the Arthurian Avalon. The actual Welsh word for the otherworld is Annwn (which is pronounced 'An-oon') and this is clearly the original that inspired the Avalon of romance.

Annwn, the spirit-world, is everywhere. We are a part of it; although we are stuck in physicality and the arrow of Time. Our ancestors, and other spirits, are ever present in Annwn. It is within all people and around all things. It is not a town in Somerset, on the A361, nine miles west of Shepton Mallet.

That said, Glastonbury is a very special and beloved place. The energy there is bright and profound; but it is just one of many places where the veil between this world and Annwn is thin. So too is the beautiful countryside of the Avallonnais in Burgundy where lies the ancient healing sanctuary by the River Cure.

It is more than probable that the 12th and 13th century people understood that Arthur was the figurehead of a Celtic pagan Mystery Tradition; written into romance to salvage their ancestral wisdom stories rather than have them destroyed as heresies. Merlin was an immaculate conception, Arthur was a Sun God, and Morgan le Fay was the benevolent goddess of a golden otherworldly realm in the furthest west; the realm of the setting sun.

A footbridge into the Avallonnais,
across the waters of the River Cousin,
below many towered Avallon.

King Arthur

From the Well Maidens of the Summerlands project

www.wellmaidens.co.uk

~ END NOTE ~

I think that it is time now for Glastonbury to up its game and to move forwards; away from repeating the same old tired Arthurian and Arimathean 'traditions'.

It is time to honour and explore Glastonbury's medieval history and its very real connections with the Angevin Empire and Avallon in France; Henry II, Eleanor of Aquitaine, Richard the Lionheart, Marie of Champagne, and the many writers of Arthurian and Grail romance that they encouraged and sponsored.

It is time to understand the Arthurian stories for what they were and still are (heretical wisdom veiled in wonderful romance); the cultural **Mysteries** of the Celtic West.

Twinning with Avallon in Burgundy would be a step in the right direction; the Glastonbury's road signs could read,

'Welcome to Glastonbury,
twinned with Avallon.'

But then again... I wont hold my breath. Maybe Avalon needs to be whatever people need it to be.

'We are but visitors on this rock,
hurtling through time and space at sixty-six thousand miles per
hour, tethered to a burning sphere by an invisible force; in an
unfathomable universe that most of us take for granted...'
(Fox Mulder, *Syzygy*, episode 13 of series 3, *The X-Files*)

Yuri Leitch
Spring Equinox
2019

~ BIBLIOGRAPHY ~

Ashe, Geoffrey; *Avalonian Quest*, Fontana, 1984.

Ashe, Geoffrey; *The Discovery of King Arthur,* Sutton Publishing, 2003.

Baring-Gould, Sabine; *Curious Myths of the Middle Ages*, New Orchard Editions, 1987.

Butler, H. E.; *The Autobiography of Gerald of Wales*, The Boydell Press, 2005

Caesar, Julius; *The Conquest of Gaul*, Penguin Classics, 1982.

Carley, James P; *Glastonbury Abbey: The Holy House at the Head of the Moors Adventurous*, Gothic Image Publications, 1996.

Collins, Andrew; *Twenty-first Century Grail*, Virgin Books, 2004.

Evans, Joan; *Life in Medieval France*, Phaidon Press, 1957.

Evans, Sebastian; (translation of) *The High History of the Holy Grail*, James Clarke & Co.

Farmer, David Hugh; *Saint Hugh of Lincoln*, Darton, Longman & Todd Ltd, 1985.

Farmer, David Hugh; *The Oxford Dictionary of Saints*, Oxford University Press, 1987.

Floyde, Marilyn; *King Arthur's French Odyssey: Avallon in Burgundy.*

Freke, Timothy and Peter Gandy; *The Jesus Mysteries*, Thorsons, 1999.

Gillingham, John; *Richard the Lionheart*, Weidenfeld & Nicolson, 1978.

Haskins, Susan; *Mary Magdalene: Myth and Metaphor*, Harcourt Brace & Company.

Llancarfan, Caradoc of; *Two Lives of Gildas*, (translated by Hugh Williams), Llanerch Enterprises, 1990.

Malmesbury, William of; *The Antiquities of Glastonbury*, (translated by Frank Lomax), J.M.F. Books, 1992.

Marcombe, David; *The Saint and the Swan: The Life and Times of St Hugh of Lincoln,* Lincoln Cathedral Publications, 2000.

Monmouth, Geoffrey of; *The History of the Kings of Britain*, (translated by Lewis Thorpe), Guild Publishing, 1982.

Monmouth, Geoffrey of; *Vita Merlini*, (translated by John Jay Parry), BiblioBazaar, 2008.

Nennius; *Nennius; British History and The Welsh Annals*, (translated by John Morris), Phillimore, 1980.

Picknett, Lynn; *Mary Magdalene: Christianity's Hidden Goddess*, Robinson, 2003.

Rankin, David and Sorita D'Este; *The Isles of the Many Gods*, Avalonia, 2007.

Spence, Lewis; *The Encyclopedia of the Occult*, Bracken Books, 1988.

Spence, Lewis; *The Fairy Tradition in Britain*, Rider and Company, 1948.

Squire, Charles; *Celtic Myth & Legend: Poetry & Romance*, Gresham, 1910.

Staines, David; *The Complete Romances of Chrétien de Troyes*, Indiana University Press, 1993.

Steele, Philip; *Encyclopedia of British History*, Miles Kelly Publishing, 2001.

Wace; *Roman de Brut*, (translated by Judith Weiss), University of Exeter Press, 2006.

Warren, W.L.; *Henry II*, University of California Press, 1977.

~ INDEX ~

THE WELL MAIDENS OF THE SUMMERLANDS

The Well Maidens of the Summerlands is an ongoing mystical and artistic project exploring the Arthurian and Celtic Mystery Traditions, sacred landscapes, and the esoteric nature of otherworld realities; which is a vast topic that is to be found stored within the whole world's ancient wisdom stories and cultural mythologies.

Yuri Leitch is a founder member of the project and he is currently working on many books and artwork (full of Mystery Tradition symbolism) to facilitate re-connection to the ancestral spirits of the Celtic lands (and all lands). As well as painting a large collection of thirty-nine 4ft high canvasses (the completed designs of which can be viewed on the Well Maidens website) Yuri is currently writing and illustrating a book about Merlin and the Thirteen Treasures of Britain.

For further information please visit

www.wellmaidens.co.uk

* * *

Made in the USA
Middletown, DE
07 May 2019